A JOURNEY OF RICHES

Transformation Calling

Published by Motion Media International
Editing: Gwendolyn Parker, Chris Drabenstott, Nicole Policarpio, Prax Yap, Amit Janco.
Cover Design: Motion Media International
Typesetting & Assembly: Motion Media International
Printing: Create Space

Creator: Spender, John - Primary Author
Title: *A Journey Of Riches - Transformation Calling*
ISBN: 978-0-6482845-2-9
Subjects: Self-Help, Autobiography and Memoirs

Acknowledgements

Writing is a gift that too few give to themselves, it is such a powerful way to reflect and gain closure from the past, writing is a therapeutic process. The experience raises ones self-esteem, confidence and awareness of ones self.

I learned this when I created the first book in the *'A Journey Of Riches'* series, which is, now one of many books in the series with over 90 different co-authors from fourteen different countries. It's not easy to write about your own personal experience's and I honour and respect everyone of the authors who has collaborated in the series thus far. For many of the authors, English is their second language, which is a major achievement within its self.

In curating this anthology of short stories, I have felt such incredible joy, and I have been inspired by the amount of generosity, gratitude, and shared energy that this experience has given everyone.

The idea for this book came to me while I was sharing the stage with my good friend Casey Plouffe, at Lenny Evan's "Follow Your Bliss" retreat in StGeorge, Utah, November 2017, I was speaking to my now good friend Adam Holzworth, about what transformation meant to him as a personal trainer and network marketer, I don't remember exactly what he said; but it inspired me to create this book about Transformation and to invite the various authors featured in this book, book nine in the best selling *A Journey of Riches* series.

Of course, I could not have created this book without the nine other co-authors who each said YES when I asked them to share their take on what transformation meant to them. Just like each chapter in this book makes inspiring reading, each story represents one chapter in the life of each of the authors.

I'd like to thank all the authors for entrusting me with their unique memories, encounters and wisdom. Thank you for sharing and opening the door to your soul, so others may learn from your experience, may the readers gleam confidence from your success's and wisdom from your failures.

Thank you to my family, I know you are proud of me and how far I have come from that 10 year old boy who was just learning how to read and write at a basic level. Mom, Robert, Dad, Merril, my brother Adam and his daughter Krystal, my sister Hollie, her partner Brian and my nephew Charlie and my niece Heidi. Also my grandparents Gran n Pop who are alive and well and Ma and Pa who now resting in peace. They accept me just the way I am with all my travels and adventures around the world.

Thanks to all the team at MotionMediaInternational who have done an excellent job at editing and collating this book. It has been a pleasure working with you all on this successful project, and I thank you for your patience in dealing with the various changes and adjustments along the way.

Thank you, the reader who has the courage to look at your life and how you can improve your future in a fast and rapidly changing world.

And I'd enjoy to connect with readers, as I love sharing stories.

You can email me here: jrspender7@gmail.com

Thank you again to my fellow co-authors: Rod Hairston, Alex Hoffmann, Katie Neubaum, Noelani Love, Jeana Matichak, Gemma Castiglia, Elizabeth Palmer, Michell Mercer, Annina Ninsk Bruhwiler.

I hope you have enjoyed, this co-authored experience as much as I have. Love and light.

Praise

"If you are looking for an inspiring read to get you through any change, this is it!! This book is filled with many gripping perspectives, from a collect of successful international authors with a tonne of wisdom to share."

~ Theera Phetmalaigul, Entrepreneur/Investor.

"*A Journey of Riches* is a remarkably inspiring collection! I was beside myself with hope and inspiration, as I read a plethora of stories written from the depths of the authors soul. It was truly uplifting to read these true stories, of people in their challenges of sorrow only to discover that there was indeed a light at the end of the tunnel.

Having been through my own struggles in life and having overcome them, it was comforting to know that there are others alike who have suffered, persevered and as a result prospered. This is a book that is a must read for anyone regardless of the trials and severity in which they have faced. A raw collection of heart wrenching experiences and moments that are sure to make you cry, laugh and curse out loud. With every piece of literature, the end result is the same; a new discovery of hope and understanding that anything can be overcome. Five stars across the board!"

~ Elise on Amazon

"*A Journey Of Riches* is an empowering series that implements two simple words in overcoming life's struggles.

By diving into the meaning of the words "problem" and "challenge," you will find yourself motivated to believe in the triumph of perseverance. With many different authors from all around the world, coming together to share different stories of life's trials, you will find yourself drenched in encouragement to push through even the darkest of battles.

The stories are personal heart felt shares of moving through and transforming challenges into rich life experiences.

The book will move, touch and inspire your spirit to face and overcome any of life's adversities. A truly inspirational read. Thank you for being the kind open soul you are John!!"

~ Casey Plouffe, Seven Figure Network Marketer.

"A must read for anyone facing major changes or challenges in life right now. This book will give you the courage to move through any challenge with confidence, grace and ease."

~ Jo-Anne Irwin - Transformational Coach & Best Selling Author.

"I'm a fan of self-help books and I read them a lot. I love this book and the stories that are contained within them, but most of all I love the concept. I love that John Spender decided to do an anthology of stories from inspirational people. This is the type of book where you can either choose to be inspired by 10 different stories or choose a chapter that resonates with you the most.

As I read this book, it confirmed to me my life suspicion that things happen in our lives we can't control. It can be extremely devastating at times. It is those moments that bring us to our knees not knowing whether we can or even want to stand anymore. But, in these challenging moments, this book confirms to me that we do have one choice we can let go, make changes and embrace the new. It's the choice of how we decide to view these hardships. Our perspective determines what our life will be after these moments in our lives.

There were some very heart wrenching stories that were contained in these books. Some of them I even had to ask myself, "How do you even recover from a situation like that?"

Perspective. It all boils down to how we decide to view those hard challenges that come our way. At least that is what I took away from this book.

Thank you to John and his team of authors for getting together to create this book."

~ Kit Zakimi on Amazon.

"This next chapter in the *A Journey of Riches* book series will inspire and motivate you to move through any challenge or change in your life! This is a must read for anyone facing major challenges right now"

~ John Newman - Founder of MyRoadtoFinancialFree-dom.com and Best Selling Author.

"A timely read as I'm facing a few changes right now. I liked the various insights from the different authors. This book will inspire you to move through any challenge or change that you are experiencing."

~ David Ostrand, Business Owner.

"I've known John Spender for a while now, I was blessed with an opportunity to be in book four in the series. I know that you will enjoy this new journey like the rest of the books in the series. The collection of stories will assist you with making changes, to deal with challenges and to see that transformation is possible for your life.

~Charlie O'shea, Entrepreneur.

"Amazing stories that remind us all that life presents us with challenges to bring out our best self. Thanks for the reminder. So inspiring and real."

~Jane Thorpe, Best Selling Author.

"Awesome! Truly inspirational! It is amazing what the human spirit can achieve and overcome! Highly recommended!!"

~Fabrice Beliard, Australian Business Coach and Best Selling Author.

"*Transformation Calling* is the ninth book in the *A Journey of Riches* book series and it is an inspirational read that will motivate you to take on any challenge in life. Make sure you grab your copy today."

~Katrina Gulabovski, Counsellor and Best Selling Author.

"The *A Journey of Riches* book series is a inspirational collection of books that will empower you to take on any challenge or change in life."

~Kay Newton, Midlife Stress Buster and Best Selling Author.

"*A Journey of Riches* book series are an inspiring collection of stories, sharing many different ideas and perspectives on how to overcome challenges, deal with change and to make empowering choices in your life. Open the book anywhere and let your mood chose where you need to read. Buy one of the books today, you'll be glad that you did! "

~Trish Rock, Modern Day Intuitive, Best selling Author, Speaker, Psychic & Holistic Coach.

"*Transformation Calling* is another inspiring read in the *A Journey of Riches* book series. The authors are from all over the world and each has a unique perspective to share, that will have you thinking differently about you're current circumstances in life. An inspiring read!"

~Alexandria Calamel, Success Coach and Best Selling Author.

"The *A Journey of Riches* books are a collection of real life stories, that are truly inspiring and give you the confidence that no matter what you are dealing with in your life, that there is a light at the end of the tunnel, and a very bright one at that.

Totally empowering!"

~ John Abbott, Freedom Entrepreneur.

"An amazing collection of true stories from individuals who have overcome great changes and who have transformed their lives and use their experience to uplift, inspire and support others."

~Carol Williams, Author-Speaker-Coach.

"You can empower yourself from the power within this book, that can help awaken the sleeping giant within you. John has a purpose in life to bring inspiring people together to share their wisdom, for the benefit of all who venture deep into this book *Transformation Calling*. If you are looking for inspiration to be someone special this book can be your guide."

~Bill Bilwani, Renown Melbourne Restaurateur.

"In *A Journey Of Riches*: *Transformation Calling*, the ninth book in the series, you will again catch the impulse to step up, re-consider and settle for only the very best for yourself and those around you. Penned from the heart and with an un-flinching drive to make a difference for the good of all, *A Journey Of Riches* series is a must-read."

~Steve Coleman Author of "*Decisions, Decisions! How to Make the Right One Every Time.*"

"If you want to be on top of your game? *A Journey of Riches* is a must read with breakthrough insights that will help you do just that!"

~ Christopher Chen, Entrepreneur.

"In *A Journey of Riches*, you will find the insight, resources and tools you need to transform your life. By reading the authors stories, you too can be inspired to achieve your greatest accomplishments and what is truly possible for you.

Reading this book activates your true potential for transforming, you're life way beyond what you think is possible. Read it and learn how you too can have a magical life."

~Elaine Mc Guinness, Best selling Author of *Unleash Your Authentic Self!*

"If you are looking for an inspiring read look no further than the *A Journey Of Riches* book series. The books are an inspiring collection of short stories, that will encourage you to embrace life even more. I highly recommend you read one of the books today!"

~Kara Dono, Doula, Healer and Best Selling Author.

"*A Journey of Riches* series is a must read for anyone seeking to enrich their own lives and gain wisdom through the wonderful stories of personal empowerment & triumphs over life's challenges. I've given several copies to my family, friends and clients to inspire and support them to step into their greatness. I highly recommend that you read these books, savoring the many aha's and tools you will discover inside."

~Michele Cempaka, Hypnotherapist, Shaman, Transformational Coach & Reiki Master.

"If you are looking for an inspirational read, look no further than the *A Journey Of Riches* book series. The books are an inspiring and educational collection of short stories from the authors soul itself, that will encourage you to embrace life even more.

I've even given them to my clients too, so that they are inspired with their journeys in life, wealth, health and everything else in between.

I recommend you make it a priority, to read one of the books today!"

~Goro Gupta, Chief Education Officer, Mortgage Terminator, Property Mentor.

"The *A Journey Of Riches* book series is filled with real-life short stories of heartfelt tribulations turned into uplifting, self-transformation by the power of the human spirit to overcome adversity. The journeys captured in these books will encourage you to embrace life in a whole new way.

I highly recommend reading this inspiring anthology series."

~Chris Drabenstott, Best Selling Author and Editor.

Table of Contents

Preface

I created this book and chose the different authors to share their personal insights, wisdom, and experiences to assist people who may be going through challenges, adversities, or changes similar to those of the authors.

Like all of us, each author has a unique story and insight to share with you. It just may be the case, that one or more of these authors have lived through an experience that is similar to circumstances in life right now and their words are the words you need to read to help you through it. Perhaps reading about one or more of these experiences will fill in the missing piece of your puzzle, so to speak. So you can move forward into the next phase on your journey.

Storytelling has been the way humankind has communicated ideas and learning throughout our civilization. While we have become more sophisticated, and life in the modern world is more convenient, there is still much discontent and dissatisfaction with one's reality. Many people have also moved away from reading books, and they are missing out on valuable information that can help them to move forward in life, with a positive outlook. I think it is important to turn off the T.V., to slow down, and to read, reflect, and take the time to appreciate everything you have in life.

I like anthology books because they carry many different perspectives and insights on a singular topic. I find that sometimes when I'm reading a book that has just one author I gain an understanding of their perspective and writing style very quickly and the reading becomes predicable. With this book and all of the books in the *'A Journey of Riches'* book series, you have many different writing styles and viewpoints that will help to shape you're own perspective with you're current set of circumstances.

Anthology books are also great because you can start from any chapter and gain a valuable insight or a nugget of wisdom without the feeling that you have missed something from the earlier chapters.

I love reading many different types of personal development books, because learning and personal growth is important to me. If you are not learning and growing, well, you're staying the same. Everything in the universe is growing, expanding, and changing. If we are not open to different ideas and different ways of thinking and being, then we can become close-minded.

The idea of this book series is to open you up to different ways of perceiving your reality, to give you hope, to give you encouragement, and to give you many avenues of thinking about the same subject. My wish for you, is to empower to make a decision that will best suit you in moving forward with your life. As Albert Einstein said, "we cannot solve problems with the same level of thinking that created them."

With Einstein's words in mind, let your mood pick a chapter in the book and allow yourself to be guided to find the answers you seek.

"Real Transformation requires real honesty. If you want to move forward - get real with yourself."

~ Bryant McGill

CHAPTER 1

Adversity (Using Adversity as a Stairway to Growth)

By Rod Hairston

"There is nothing either good or bad, but thinking makes it so."

– Hamlet, William Shakespeare

Our brains have the magnificent ability to assign meaning to every experience we have. We have the capability and the imagination to allow us to measure every experience in our lives and evaluate them as good or bad. These evaluations are based on the beliefs we hold about ourselves, how the world works, our self-esteem, and our environments.

The true beauty in this is that we have the power to assign the meaning that we know will best serve us and our growth. As long as we are alive, every experience we have can be turned into value for ourselves and for others. The challenge is in learning how to do this.

For every experience someone has that they recognize as adversity, someone else will experience the same situation as a blessing. Adversity is always an opportunity. It may not immediately feel like it, but honing the skill of being able to reframe and redefine adversity, either in the moment or in hindsight, allows you to turn all adversity, big and small, into opportunity.

No life is without adversity, and yet the ways people react to adversity can make or break them.

As a Second Class Petty Officer in the Navy at 19 years old, I was advancing quickly through the ranks and earning high marks in every review. A new Senior Chief came in and over time, my marks started to drop. I was still working as hard as ever and doing my best, but my marks got lower and lower with each review.

I began to doubt myself. Maybe I wasn't smart enough after all. Maybe I'd fooled my previous leaders and now someone saw the real truth about me. Maybe I was never good enough for this role.

As I saw my friends, even those I knew were screw ups, receiving higher marks and reviews while mine continued to drop, I gave up. I stopped showing up to trainings as early. I stopped working so hard. I believed the marks were a true reflection of who I was as a 20-year-old man.

Finally, one of my friends came to me and confided that he'd been going out for drinks with the Senior Chief and he had learned that the Senior Chief didn't think a young black guy should be getting the kinds of marks I'd been getting. So he was sabotaging me. Whether he was doing it intentionally or not, no matter how hard I worked, I would not get recognized for it. And here I was playing perfectly into his racist beliefs.

I realized that I had to just be myself. I couldn't let this guy's racism change how I knew I could and should be doing my job. So I started working hard again. I started being great again, and I didn't care what the marks said about me because I knew they weren't true.

Eventually, the Commander called the Senior Chief and me into his office over the bad marks I'd continued to receive. He was disappointed in me and told me that he'd talked me up so much to the new Senior Chief; he couldn't believe how I'd let him down.

He told me to do whatever I needed to do to get my marks back up, and he told the Senior Chief – the guy who had been giving me horrible marks even when I was doing a great job again – that he was holding him accountable to make sure my marks came back up, too.

Before I knew it, my marks were back where they had been and continued to get even better. The Senior Chief respected me for not falling victim to the adversity he had challenged me with and we eventually became really good friends.

This was one of the key moments in my life when I recognized that the short-term effects of adversity do not define you. You do not have to let them change your identity and who you know yourself to be. I allowed the adversity, the challenge of it all, to impact me at first. I believed the marks reflected who I was, and I had no power to change them. My superior officer didn't think someone of my race could succeed, and I can't control my race, so I had no control over the situation I was in.

But I did have the power to stay true to myself. I realized the real opportunity was in taking the adversity and using it to grow and to reinforce my own identity.

Ultimately, there will always be someone who views you differently than you view yourself; someone who thinks you can't succeed or shouldn't succeed, whether that's due to your race, gender, sexual preference, education level, or any other variety of characteristics. If you look for those people and focus on their beliefs about you, you will always find them.

What you focus on, you find, and it seems real. Once you believe that someone else is right, you have fallen into the trap of doubting yourself and sabotaging your own success.

In my case, the Senior Chief's racism was his own pattern for interacting with the world. If I played into his pattern, I was the only one who got hurt. I realized his beliefs were ignorant, and if I spent time being hurt about it or internalizing it, his ignorance was never going to change.

By ignoring his efforts to sabotage my success, by being true to the identity I had of myself as an excellent sailor, I took away the power his beliefs had over me. Nobody is more powerful than my own ability to create my own destiny, and I am very fortunate to have learned this lesson as a young man.

Sometimes in life, you have to go deeper than other people to achieve the same results. There will always be someone smarter, faster, and richer and someone with a better relationship, a nicer house, and smarter kids. But when you choose to turn adversity into an opportunity for something bigger, you still cultivate the life you want to create, even if you have to work a bit harder for it.

Out of this friendship with the Senior Chief and working hard to make my commander acknowledge my work ethic and be proud of me again, I was able to have one of the proudest experiences in my life. Because of my outstanding record in the Navy, I was nominated as one of the top 1% to enter into the Enlisted Education Advancement Program, which allowed me to get a college degree while being a paid member of the Navy. I didn't have to do NROTC while I was in school. Getting my education and finishing my degree was my job for four years.

I was able to take the adversity of a racist Senior Chief and turn it into an opportunity to not only gain a friend who valued me and my contributions beyond the color of my skin, but also to get my education paid for. I had never believed myself to be college material before I was nominated for the Enlisted Education Advancement Program. I went into the Navy because I didn't believe I could do much else, and ironically, the Navy helped me see how much I really could overcome.

Instead of allowing adversity to get to me, to label me as someone who didn't deserve to succeed no matter how hard I tried, I realized at that point that adversity can in fact be the greatest gift in life. My experience in the Navy gave me the knowledge that adversity can make you better. Adversity doesn't define you unless you allow it to.

Once I left the Navy and became a master trainer for Tony Robbins, I realized how truly emotionally strong I am. I was able to take my own experiences of adversity and use the insight that I had gained to help people who were depressed and suicidal.

At any given Tony Robbins event, there are thousands and thousands of people who want to work with him and be part of his training team. It's very, very hard to become a trainer in his organization. I attended an event with a friend to learn how to sell, and he picked me out of the crowd to talk to. I don't know what he saw in my eye contact or body language, but he chose me, not only to talk to as part of the event, but he told me to meet with him afterwards and invited me to join his team as a trainer.

You have to endure a lot to become a trainer with Tony – ridiculously long hours, tons of travel, very emotionally and mentally exhausting events. When I joined the team, I knew he saw some mental and emotional strength in me, and this was reinforced when he mentored me to quickly move through the ranks.

After two years, I was promoted from a trainer to a master trainer, skipping over a level in the organization. There were people coming to the events from all over the world looking for support and strength, and Tony wanted me in a position of leadership among the trainers.

Working through all the challenges and obstacles to get to that level in my career allowed me to have the incredible opportunity to reframe and redefine adversity for not only thousands of adults at events, but also for kids.

Tony tapped me to run his first Discovery Camp, a seven-day mastery event designed for youth from ages 13-18. The event focused on self love, self esteem and leadership. For the first event, we had no agenda, no training curriculum, and no real program to deliver, and he handed it over to me to execute. I had to rally the other trainers around me after just coming from a huge and exhausting Life Mastery event to create a program on the fly. That first event went so well, we quickly scheduled a bigger one in Lake Tahoe, which was even more successful. Troubled kids were transforming, and their parents were raving about what an impact we'd had on their children in just a week.

After our third event to work out the kinks, the program was officially born, and it continues to this day as an impactful program for kids. We helped kids from over 19 countries, usually about 1100 kids at each event, and I love knowing that my team and I created every aspect of that camp based on the adversities that each of us had overcome in our own lives.

There was one young man in particular whose breakthrough has always stayed with me. It was our third Discovery Camp event, and we were starting to get a lot of attention and people who wanted to be a part of it. These volunteers from all over the world always joined us with the best of intentions to help support the kids, but they approached it the way many people would; they wanted to avoid any adversity in the camp. Although they recognized that the kids were there for a breakthrough, they just wanted to focus on love and how amazing the kids could be without acknowledging the deep experiences that had brought them to a troubled time in their young lives.

One of the cops in particular wanted to eject this young man. The kid was 15 years old and would show up to sessions late, sometimes smelled like he'd been smoking pot, kept his feet casually propped up on a chair, and seemed to enjoy pushing the boundaries of acceptable behavior. He never did anything to hurt other kids or that was clearly bad enough to be kicked out, but he was always seeking negative attention and generally being annoying.

Finally, a group of adults were encouraging me to kick him out of the program, arguing that we needed to set an example for the other kids and show them that we wouldn't let him create that much disturbance in the camp setting. I asserted that he was exactly the kind of kid we'd designed the camp for, but after three days of his distracting behavior, I was worn down. He was disruptive, had gone into other kids' rooms without permission, and was a lot of work. I decided we would try to reach him with one more exercise and if that didn't work, he would have to leave camp.

We did a process with all the kids asking them to close their eyes and visit their past selves, explore their present belief systems and the limitations they currently held, and then create new belief systems for their future selves. Kids' imaginations are so incredibly powerful, and magical thinking is common, so this was a very impactful exercise, usually involving a lot of tears, breakthroughs, and celebration once the limiting beliefs were released.

This day, we were sharing about the negative and limiting beliefs that many kids were releasing, and some were bringing things they no longer needed or wanted up to the stage

– drugs, heroin needles, razor blades for self-mutilation. This one young man stayed seated with his head down, and it was obvious that he was genuinely affected by the exercise. Until this moment, nothing at the camp had broken through his tough guy act; everything had been treated as if it was funny or silly or useless.

In this moment, when someone approached him with a microphone, asking him to share what he was processing, all he could say through his tears was, "It's not my fault, is it?"

I asked him what wasn't his fault, and he shared that his parents had gotten divorced when he was eight years old. He would go to his dad's house on the weekends to watch sports with him and each week, he saw his dad get more down, more unhappy, more sad, more depressed.

One week he showed up at his dad's house and his dad was surprised. There was plastic over the furniture, and his dad asked him why he was there. He said he was there to watch the game, so his dad told him to go get him a beer from the kitchen.

As he walked into the kitchen, he heard a gunshot and turned back around to see that his dad has just shot himself in the head and died.

This young man spent half his life thinking his father hated him so much that he'd shot himself right in front of him. He believed he made his dad so unhappy that he had to kill himself just to get away from his own son. Through this Discovery Camp exercise, he finally realized that he had nothing to do with his father's suicide and it wasn't his fault.

He had a massive breakthrough about the adversity he'd experienced at such a young age, and everyone in the room felt it. The cop who had advocated so strongly to have him removed recognized that the adversity he'd brought into the camp sessions was simply a coping mechanism for how he dealt with the conflict that he'd internalized so many years ago. After this breakthrough, everything changed – his eyes changed, his face changed, even his complexion changed. He was free of the burden of this adversity when he realized that he had no control over it, other than the ability to reframe it.

Overcoming adversity requires a lot of courage. You have to be courageous to develop the right thinking in preparation for the adversity that you're not anticipating or expecting. There are times when you enter a situation and know you may be challenged or you may face adversity, such as when you move to a new town or leave a job, but often times, adversity is unexpected. In developing the courage you need to face that adversity, you also increase your emotional strength and increase your ability to lead and support other people through their own uncertainty and adversity.

At this stage in my life, I see adversity as a choice. I can always choose to feed certain response patterns by focusing on specific emotions and beliefs that the adverse experience brings up. Or, I can choose to ignore those patterns and focus on how I want my life to be after I have overcome whatever adversity is currently in my path.

There will always be adversity in life if I choose to focus on it. Instead, I view it simply as a contrast to all the joy, happiness, and success I have in my life. Rather than trying to get rid of or avoid adversity, I embrace the choice to recognize all the value that it brings to my life. I express gratitude and joy for that spotlight on the contrast. I consistently look at the challenges in my life and then make a decision on how I can reframe them to better serve me and my goals. Making this choice over and over has helped me to mature into a better person, a better man, and a better leader.

Throughout my life, I have had some great role models on how to deal with adversity, and some less than great role models. On the one hand, my mother would regularly fall into a victim mindset and take whatever she was dealing with out on her children and other people in life whenever she was faced with adversity. This was particularly difficult to deal with because she came from a place of pure intent; she never intended to pass the burden of her challenges on to the people she loved, but we all felt it nonetheless, and had to deal with it in our own unique ways.

On the other hand, my grandfather was quite an inspiring role model for dealing with life's challenges. He would constantly tell vivid stories to make his adversaries human, to view his challenges in a different light that gave them a more manageable perspective. When he was faced with racism, he would tell me that "you don't have to let people take advantage of you, but before you judge someone, you always have to check to see if they're an angel bringing you some other lesson or perspective you didn't expect". He taught me that angels come in all colors, shapes, and sizes, and the lessons are often hidden. So before I could accuse someone of being racist or prejudiced, before I could become the victim in any interaction, I first had to assume they were an angel trying to show me something bigger or better about myself or the world in general.

Learning to approach adversity by reframing the story about what I needed to hear helped me minimize the impact that these adverse experiences had on my life. If you have the courage to tell the story differently, to see it differently, it's inevitably going to make you stronger.

Like every great movie, every great life has adversity in it and people who are steadily overcoming it. A weak movie or story includes adversity that the hero can't overcome – the lesson isn't learned and the adversity emerges as the winner. As a viewing audience, we don't enjoy those stories because they feel too much like real life. Too often in our daily lives, we experience people who struggle with their adversity only to fall in defeat to it. But when we see someone who has the courage, faith, and persistence to overcome adversity, to tell a story about those experiences that allows them to reframe and conquer the challenges, we want to celebrate and model those people. We call them heroes and want to share their inspiring stories of overcoming adversity with the world.

Life is about being able to adapt and overcome. It's not the strongest and the fastest creatures or people who always win; it's the creatures and people who can adapt to their circumstances, who can overcome the challenges we all experience in life, and who use that adversity to build their strength in order to tell a different story.

Too much of the time, people look at the world around them and allow the fear to take over. We spend our lives worried about the what ifs, staying with what we know because at least we're surviving, even if we're not thriving. We are afraid to adapt. We fight for our old ways of living and being because it's what we know.

When we say as a nation that we want to get back to being great, we are essentially saying that we refuse to learn from adversity. We refuse to learn from the adversity that comes from change, the adversity that comes from breaking the old patterns of behavior that keep us trapped where we are and believing that that's all we deserve to have. We would rather take the world down with us than to admit we could approach things differently and do the hard work to reframe the adversity into an opportunity.

The people who refuse to learn, who refuse to grow and change from the adversity in the world will not survive. They will become obsolete.

Some people believe they have to have the adversity in order to change and grow, and that hitting a crisis is necessary before they can do things differently. They may even unconsciously create crises in order to make the changes they desire without even realizing they're doing it. They need the adversity as a catalyst.

One of the most beautiful things in life is the ability to anticipate the adversity that is inevitable. When you proactively open your mind, you can more easily anticipate adversity without self-judgment. If you anticipate adversity, you can use it.

A sailboat that is not prepared for the winds to change can find itself in a very adverse situation when the storm arrives. Sailors who understand weather patterns and know how quickly they can change are more able to adjust their sails and move faster through the storms.

Ultimately, adversity is not necessarily positive or negative. It just is. It's adverse to the way things are going, and it can often lead you in a much better direction if you are open to viewing the story through that lens. The ability to anticipate adversity requires you to be non-judgmental, to be curious, and to be able to deal with uncertainty. You have to know that the only constant in life is change. When you can anticipate that, you are more able to handle whatever adversity comes your way.

One of the greatest gifts or abilities in life is to be able to find the humor in adversity. When you consider some of the greatest comedians in the world, they are people who took massive adversity – abuse, addictions, mental illness – and turned it around into something that created humor. These comedians have looked at racism, inequality, illness, and pain and learned how to laugh at them all. Then they shared that laughter and perspective with the world.

Humor allows adversity to become silly and to lose some of the overwhelming power that it can hold over you. It helps us to realize that adversity is not based on anything more than our own viewpoint of it and the value we assign to it as negative or bad. If you can find humor in adversity, you have discovered the essence of happiness. Being able to adapt to adversity and find the humor in it is the greatest tool in overcoming it.

One of the most adverse and most difficult experiences I've had to handle recently was the death of my ex-wife to cancer. She was someone I loved and cared about for a long time, and she was sick for many years. When our marriage ended, we continued to raise our children together and always wanted the best for each other. Then she got sick, and I had to watch her succumb to that adversity, and not only process my own feelings about it, but also help our children prepare to lose their mother, who was very special to them. I knew they had to learn how to handle and deal with the adversity they were experiencing, too. I had to help them anticipate how to approach each day with the ups and downs of her treatment, knowing I was ultimately not responsible for her health or their responses to it.

In so many situations, you may think you see what's going on in someone's life, yet truly have no idea what's happening underneath or inside. For my own life, I am always asking if I am being congruent with what I teach and what I say I believe. When I see adversity as a fork in the road, I know I have a choice as to which road I will take to deal with it. Unfortunately, so many people never even realize that the fork exists and that they do in fact have a choice.

Adversity truly gives you the gift of being able to reframe any situation and make that choice. You can decide to develop the courage to handle any situation and rewrite the story with love and gratitude for the lessons it provides for you, or you can decide to stay in a victim mentality and let the adversity happen to you. When you make the first choice, adversity becomes a stairway to the next level of your growth as a person.

Adversity presents itself as a contrast to true love and joy and happiness. You can sit in a moment of adversity and know that what came before and what came after is what is true because you see the difference and know the adversity is something you can and will overcome. Adversity is a mirror to your growth; it's sometimes hard to see and appreciate all that you have grown through if you avoid or deny the adversity that helped you to get there.

Through seeing my ex-wife's experience and death from cancer and helping our kids learn how to process that adversity from their own perspectives, I was reminded of how great a strength it is to reframe adversity and instead tell a story that supports the vision I have for my life.

There are certain questions I often ask myself when I am faced with adversity, as I look at that fork in the road: I'm here, and I'm alive and well, so what is this trying to teach me? How will I use what I learn from this adversity to help other people? Do my current beliefs about myself and my strength support me getting through this? What new beliefs and references do I need to build to get through this experience? Who can I use as a role model for how to get through this beautifully? What strength, power, or gift is this adversity helping me to shape and refine in my life?

Adversity makes the story of my life stronger – the story that I have already lived through and everything I am creating ahead of me. I know I will continue to have adversity in my life, and I welcome and accept it with gratitude and humor because of the gift it is to me. When you anticipate adversity and reframe the experience to tell a story that doesn't involve being a victim to your experiences, you can discover the true essence of yourself that can support you when adversity comes.

Regardless of what happens when adversity hits, the knowledge of your own ability to reframe and draw on that essence is the stairway to the true gift in any adversity.

"There is nothing in a caterpillar
that tells you it's going
going to be a butterfly."

~ Bucky Fuller

CHAPTER 2

Transformation is a Journey

By John Spender

False Start

I hadn't seen some of my high school buddies for over 20 years and I was excited to catch up with a few of the boys. I was one of the only ones there that weren't drinking, and after a few rounds, some of the boys started opening up. Craig, who I went to school with from the 1st grade at Kanwal Public School all the way to year 11 at Gorokan High School on the Central Coast. He started telling me how proud he was of me. But when he told his dad who he was catching up with, his dad was surprised. "Is that the same John Spender that hit a cricket ball through our lounge room window?" Before he could continue with my long list of offences, Craig chirped up and told him that I'm now an international best-selling author, producing a movie documentary about the benefits of having adversity in your life, and that I'm now living in Bali committed to helping others.

His Dad said, "For sure, I thought that kid was going to jail. He was out of control and always up to no good."

It was quite emotional for me to hear an old friend from my school days share his dad's perspective about how far off the rails I had gone. It was awesome to really get a sense of how much I had transformed my life and how people in that environment gave me no chance in their mind of living a successful life, a life that I'm proud to show up for every day. I never really saw myself as a bad kid. I rolled with the cool group at school, and I did get into drugs and alcohol at an early age, but I always had a part-time job after school, either delivering pamphlets, the local paper, collecting shopping trolleys or delivering milk, and eventually stacking shelves at the local supermarket. I just hung out with kids that were always up to bad shit; everything from stealing home brew, to shop lifting, smoking bongs, bullying other kids, getting into punch-ups, eventually taking acid trips and injecting speed.

I felt trapped in this environment and I wasn't sure what to do. Should I continue into year 11? Most of my friends had left school and were either working in apprenticeships or as laborers. My environment wasn't healthy for me anymore and the best thing that happened to me was that, after year 11, I started a Pathways School Program, which meant I had to repeat year 11 and complete year 12. The main focus was Horticulture with Math, English, and Geography as the main regular subjects. I was excited to begin afresh on a blank canvas, so to speak. I began to focus, and I became determined to do really well at school. Those two years of dedication laid the foundation for future success in business. I worked hard, and I made many sacrifices to get good grades while working part-time as a landscape laborer. After I completed school, I landed a job as an apprentice landscape gardener during a time when it was difficult to gain employment, as Australia was in a recession. After two years of working hard, one year as an apprentice the other as a laborer, I started my own business, and before I knew it, I was living in an amazing apartment overlooking Double Bay and the city, earning more money than I knew how to manage. We were mostly doing large soft landscaping projects for Randwick Council, and leading up to the Sydney Olympics, business was booming.

The Illusion of Success

My oldest uncle on my mother's side of the family was a real rogue. I had looked up to him ever since I was a little boy. He had a successful property business and lived in a mansion right on the water between Chinamans Beach and Balmoral Beach in Mosman on the North Shore of Sydney. Quite often I would spend time at his and my auntie's place looking after my younger cousins. They even took me on holidays to the Gold Coast. They lived an amazing life, and it was magical to have a taste of it. Life with my mom meant working and saving for everything in our lives, and at times we were dirt poor, wearing second-hand clothes.

I remember my step-dad used to drive the bulldozer at the local dump, and he would bring home bike parts and make second-hand bikes. The whole family had second-hand bikes from the dump.

My local soccer club, the Kanwal Rovers, were looking to raise money to run the club. They put on a raffle, and sponsors had donated a BBQ and an outdoor dining set as the first prize. It was a dollar a ticket, and whoever sold the most tickets won a brand new red ten-speed racing bike. As soon as I saw that bike, I knew I was going to do whatever it took to win. We had two months to sell as many tickets as possible. I was 11 turning 12 at the time, and I went door-to-door selling raffle tickets to local businesses and in the evening to sporting matches to sell the tickets. After selling a book of ten tickets, we would take the money back to the club treasurer, Mrs. Jefferies, and collect another set of tickets. After a while, she trusted me with a block of ten books, and it was down to me and one other kid who had sold 11 sets of tickets, and I had sold nine. After spending the weekend at my uncle's place, I gathered the courage to ask him if he would buy some raffle tickets. After I explained to him that whoever sold the most tickets would win a racing bike, he bought six books. That was sixty dollars worth back in 1988. Winning that bike at that time in my life was a proud moment, and I just thought the world of my uncle. I learned that you need to work hard for success, and it also helps to know people who can give you a helping hand.

After I had won the bike and I told him the whole story, my dad explained to me and my two siblings that our mother's side of the family wasn't the best, and he told us about the various family members who had been to jail, including my favorite uncle who had done time for armed robbery. I was shocked, but I still looked up to him and the lifestyle he lived.

Fast forward to 1997 when my business was doing well. My uncle had almost gone bankrupt, was divorced twice, and had started a small real estate firm that wasn't doing so well. I was giving him part-time work and he was staying at my place until he could land another big deal. I would do anything for my uncle. I remember when he spent two weeks in jail for getting caught drunk driving for the ninth time. I went to visit, and I was strip-searched. I couldn't understand why. I just came to give my uncle some money and told him the bad news that his wife didn't want anything to do with him and she was going to light a candle for his safety. It was shattering news as they had a newborn girl and he just wanted to be with his family. This was about the time that I learned what he had done before he was a property developer; he had been a drug trafficker and mastermind behind moving large qualities of marijuana around Australia. He had used that money along with his first wife's family wealth to run a large exclusive property development company.

In no time at all, I was buying large qualities of drugs with my savings from my business and going out partying with my uncle and his friends. I was a terrible dealer, and, like my uncle, I had a lot of unresolved issues from the past. Looking back now, I was self-medicating on a cocktail of cocaine, ecstasy, alcohol... Anything I could get my hands on, I would take it. I would take so much cocaine that it would fall out of my nose, and many times I would past out. The women that I attracted were mostly strippers, and I was getting into lots of fights.

One particular night, I was partying with some friends in Manly and I was dirty dancing with a couple of hot women. Some homie-looking guy was dancing with his friends and kept digging his shoulder into me. I would turn around and he would apologize and then laugh with his friends, only to do it again. In that situation you just try to ignore them, right? But the last straw was when he poured his drink on me. I turned around and king hit him, sitting him on his ass. The bouncer kicked me out, and the girls came with me to another bar. After that bar had closed, one of the girls was going to come home with me.

As we were waiting for a taxi, the guy that I had king hit earlier in the night was now standing in front of me with his mates, and they wanted revenge. I yelled at them, saying let's go one-on-one. They motioned that we would go around the corner, and I knew it wasn't going to be a fair fight. There were four of them and me. I thought my best chance here was to fight them out in the open, and if I couldn't take them all, that someone might break it up. Outnumbered, I knew I had to strike first. I launched a flying head-butt, and I connected right on the side of the face of the guy who had started the earlier fight. There was blood everywhere, and he was out cold on the ground. I immediately started to get stuck into the next closest guy, when a group of bouncers came to my aid, broke up the fight, and told me to get out of there.

I went into the lane to take a piss and I turned around to see about 15 men all wanting to have a go, and it was on again. Lucky for me the cops had arrived, and they arrested me and not the other guys. My uncle had always told me that if I was ever arrested then I should say nothing and get a lawyer. Little did I know at the time that all I had to do was to tell my side of the story and that would have been the end of it. Instead, I was charged with assault causing grievous bodily harm and a court date was set. I was proven not guilty and let off. I did lie, though, denying that I had headbutted the guy. There was no way that I was going to get a criminal record for defending myself.

I continued dealing, partying, getting into more fights... Things were getting worse. I was out partying at the Icebox nightclub in Kings Cross on a Sunday night with another friend of mine who was a successful drug dealer, meaning he was actually making money. We were both off our heads on a mix of cocaine, pills, and alcohol. We were having a blast and it was around 4 a.m. when I decided to call it a night. I thought I had left my jacket on a seat and I accused a guy of stealing it, and we started punching on. All his friends got involved, and the fight continued outside. My friend found my jacket next to his in the locker room where you put your jacket before you enter the club. My buddy managed to placate the other guys, and I was told to get out of there before they shot me.

I was so out of it, and I left the scene quickly. As I was walking down the road trying to flag a cab, I noticed a group of guys following me down the street. They were yelling out to me from about 400 yards away. I ran into Bear Park which is just down from Kings Cross. I ran through the park and into a construction site for a park-side home. I grabbed a metal pole and I waited behind the back wall ready to swing the pole at the first fucker that stuck his head around the corner. Unexpectedly, nobody came, so I walked around to the front of the house facing the park, and I thought I could see some guys zig-zagging through the park hiding from one tree to the next. I decided, armed with the pole, I would run out to meet them, but when I arrived no one was there. Was I seeing things? I still wasn't sure, so I continued to walk to my apartment in Edgecliff with the pole in one hand. As I made my way up the road, I felt it was safe enough to ditch the pole. I was almost home when the sun began to rise, and I noticed that a couple of men were running up the street from one side of the road to another. I ran to my garage and grabbed my chainsaw and ran out to greet them, only to find out that it was two men running behind a truck collecting people's trash. That should have been the straw that broke the camel's back, but it wasn't. I continued down the same path.

I remember doing a deal at a guy's place, and I was so paranoid that I was wearing leather gloves as I handed him an ounce of cocaine and he just looked at me like, "Who the fuck are you?" I just laughed and said, "You can't be too careful these days." Many people in that world thought I was an uncover cop. One time I was outside a nightclub and a friend of mine started raking up lines of cocaine on top of his car and telling me to snort it in front of some Kings Cross heavy underworld figures. I snorted both lines. Everyone laughed, and all was good. There were so many red flags that I was in over my head, but I was like a moth drawn to a street light, and I couldn't get enough of this lifestyle.

My uncle and I went halves on a large shipment of cocaine, and he said he had a buyer lined up ready to purchase. I met my uncle and his friend, who was known to be a real dangerous criminal, known to have committed many murders. (He is now in jail.) I'll call him Mr. X. He had even done time in a notorious London prison where he came out of the isolation unit and was attacked from behind with an iron bar by someone wanting to make a name for themselves by taking out The Mr. X. We met in a famous Indian restaurant, sat down and ate one of the most delicious Indian meals I've ever had and discussed the plan for the deal. It turned out that the Federal police had us under surveillance and were watching our every move. I'm not sure what happened exactly, but the deal didn't go through, and I had given my uncle a lot of cash. Mr. X was blaming my uncle for the Feds tailgating us, following us everywhere we went, and even helicopters buzzing around the apartment.

My uncle said he had another buyer, and he went with Mr. X to do the deal. It was an old friend of his and he gave the guy the drugs without the money. He came back with some story, saying he'll have it next week. What I later found out was he only gave half to his friend and he continued to use and sell the rest, keeping the money, and Mr. X took his share as well. I confronted my uncle about this. (We were still living together at the time.) He had been into the coke, and he started to go crazy at me. I told him how disappointed I was in him, that he was a disgrace and a bum. I went to my room and closed the door. About 15 minutes later, he started screaming at my door, calling me all these names and saying that he was going to kill me. He kicked the door open and came charging in at me, armed with a bottle and a knife. He charged into my room throwing the bottle as he ran towards me. The bottle missed me and crashed against the wall. He then tried to stab me in the face with the large knife. Ducking under his strike, I sidestepped him. We both stopped. He started calling me a coward and all sorts of profanities, everything under the sun. I dropped to my knees I began slapping my forehead really hard, and I screamed at him to do it. Looking back now, part of me wanted to die. My life was a mess. That was the end of it and he stormed out of my room.

Subsequently, I lost all my major contracts and moved back to my mom's place to get away from all the drama. I was a mess, and kicking my drug habit was hard. The only way that I knew how to get off the drugs was to isolate myself from the crowd that I had been associating with in that period of my life. I was only 23 years of age, and it took me about five years before I gained the confidence to operate another successful legitimate business. I began to see less and less of my uncle, and he no longer had any influence over me. Mr. X is now spending the rest of his life in prison for master-minding a shipment of 250 kilograms of cocaine into Australia. My other friends are either dead, behind bars, or have moved on. I wasn't cut out to be a drug dealer at all and that is one of my proudest failures. I continued to take drugs on and off until the 26th of January, Australia Day 2010.

My transformation was a slow one. I suffered from anxiety attacks and depression, and I would drink alcohol every day of the week while maintaining a successful landscaping business and traveling whenever I could. My nervous system was shot from the drug-taking and excessive drinking - and I would quit all the abusive substances only to get back on it again.

I was struggling to come to terms with a number of emotionally significant events that had happened to me as a child. When I was seven I was picked up by my ankles and pole driven into my own feces by my mother's boyfriend. I had gone to the bathroom at the last minute because my favorite show on T.V., and I was waiting for a commercial break. I hadn't realized that a nugget of poo had fallen onto the floor, and the guy went to the toilet not long after me and stepped in it. That was an extremely dramatic experience for me, and it taught me to be strong and determined in life.

Another incident that took some 20-odd years to come to terms with was when a different uncle and I were wrestling in the lounge room. There was family around, and the adults were having a few drinks. My uncle pinned me to the floor and pulled my pajama pants down. I was trying hard to stop him while our family was sitting, watching, and laughing. He then grabbed an ice cube and stuck it in my bum. Naturally, I was shocked. I looked to my family, and they thought it was so funny and burst out with laughter. I felt grossly violated and confused, how was that okay? Sometimes people do creepy things, and it's best not to dwell in the past.

The thing for me was, I just didn't know how to process or express my feelings. That was the era where kids should be seen, not heard, and if something bad happened, we should just sweep it under the mat and pretend that it had never happened at all. Well, we live, learn, and hopefully have the courage to confront the past, face it, and move on to a positive way of living life so as not to repeat the past.

The Epiphany

After an epic adventure snowboarding in Italy and partying in the Canary Islands, I was out celebrating Australia Day at the Bondi Hotel in Eastern Suburbs of Sydney with a mate of mine. He had a bag of cocaine and we were doing lines in the toilet. I went to the sink to wash my face and to snort a little bit of water to clean my nose. I looked up into the mirror and thought to myself, "What the fuck am I doing?" I didn't like the party scene anymore; it was too shallow and superficial. I looked at my reflection and I hated what I was doing, but I couldn't stop it either. I despised myself. After that moment, I made a decision to transform my life forever. I didn't know how, but I knew that I couldn't go on living this way. Sometimes you come to that moment in life where enough is enough and you just have to change. That's when you know you are ready for transformation. I wanted to have a deeper meaning to my life. I wanted a life with purpose and wanted to do something that made life easier for other people.

I joined an expensive year-long coaching program with the goal of becoming a life coach, and I began changing who I associated with, and then my circle of friends changed completely. I stopped going out and I stopped buying beer after work. I stopped drinking alcohol. Beer was a little more challenging, as it was so conditioned into my subconscious mind. I intuitively found a solution, and that was to substitute beer with ginger beer, and that worked. Casually I will have a beer, but just one or two at most. I just don't like the feeling of being drunk so much. I like to feel in control of my life. I stopped having sex and went celibate for 11 months, and that was harder than I thought it would be. But after a while I felt edgy and moody and uncomfortable in my own skin. I just wanted to push my boundaries in a healthy way.

I needed to gain some momentum for my own personal transformation. I now believe in moderation, and my actions are more based on experiences I want to live rather than feeling as if I don't have a choice. I just know that my life is better when I don't drink alcohol and I eat healthy food. Over time I've set goals, and I gradually release a layer of behavior that doesn't serve me. And I transform another aspect of my life and how I show up. Transformation in reality—at least in my life—has been a step-by-step journey, and after a period of time it appears to be a dramatic change, like that of a caterpillar morphing into a beautiful butterfly. We see this as a phenomenal transformation, and we forget that there was a period of time when the caterpillar was in a cocoon. This is the transition period that people don't see, and this is the time to be patient with ourselves. Human transformation is a journey. It's a continuation process that doesn't stop until we leave our body and transition into a new existence. We are in constant transformation. No matter if we are resistant to change, it is going to happen anyway, so you might as well consciously choose the direction that you are heading in life.

I don't know what transformation means to you. I do know what has helped me on my journey to transform from a wounded, angry, drug-taking fool who changed skill sets completely into a man of integrity, kindness, and empathic to others. I have transitioned into life coaching, speaking, becoming an NLP trainer in Southeast Asia, to organically moving into publishing, creating the *A Journey of Riches* book series, helping other ordinary people like you and me to share personal stories about change, challenge, choices, and transformation. This has shown me the strength of the human spirit and has highlighted how resilient people are when dealing with adversity.

Changes that Support Transformation

***Environment:** Changing your environment is a major key to transforming your current set of circumstances and behaviors. I'm sure you have heard of the saying "monkey see monkey do." A similar pattern is evident in us as well, because all behavior is learned behavior. We are conditioned to be a certain way, first by our parents and then by the world around us. If you take a baby at birth from Indonesia and give the baby to parents in Madagascar, that baby will be conditioned to the life of the parents in Madagascar. The child will speak the language of the parents and will model the character straits and behaviors of its parents and surroundings.

If you want to become a life coach, your first step is to surround yourself with other aspiring and successful life coaches or read books and watch videos on what successful people are doing in the field that you wish to be good in. Then you want to do, to take action. This will get your flying hours up. Repetition is the mother of all skill, as Malcom Caldwell wrote in his best-selling book, *Outliners,* researching and discovering, mastery of anything takes around 10,000 hours. Modelling and associating with others that have the skill set and the success you are seeking is a sure way to elevate your transformation.

***Stop it:** Quitting the actives and the behaviors that no longer serve your greater good is a big step towards transforming your life in a positive way. So often we do the same things and expect a different result, mostly because of the fear of the unknown. It feels safer to do the same old same old. A few things that I either reduced or stopped completely are

i) T.V. I've pretty much stopped watching T.V. In fact, I don't even own one anymore. This has allowed me to be far more productive. I do watch YouTube, and 95% of what I watch are self-improvement videos to keep reminding me why I'm doing what I'm doing and to course correct if needed. I also read personal development books and I just finished *Say it like Obama and Win,* by Shell Leanne, a great book on developing your skills as a leader and speaker.

ii) Another one that I'm still working on is being late; to show up on time for friends and appointments. How you do anything is how you do everything, and this is something that I'm developing. I believe it shows how committed you are to your friends and what you are working on. Being on time is the ultimate display of integrity and responsibility for yourself and how you show up for others.

iii) Stop socializing with people who don't appreciate you or see your full potential. Life is just too short to accept anything less. This was a hard one for me to manage. It just seemed that, no matter how hard I tried to make new friends, I would always attract the same type of party people. It wasn't until I made a whole-hearted decision to change myself and my life that I began to attract friends who saw my value and truly respected me for Me. A good exercise that helped me a great deal was to grab a sheet of paper and to list the character traits that I most admire in people that I look up to, and I started to notice that I was able to demonstrate the same traits they possessed. Also, I found that doing what I said I was going to do increased my self-image, my self-esteem, and my confidence. Then my belief in myself went up, knowing that I could do anything I put my mind to achieving.

iv) Stop with procrastinating. This is another ongoing challenge for me. This might surprise some people who know me, as I get a lot done. I don't procrastinate as much as I use to, but I'm still aware that I do, and now I just stack the deck in my favor. For example, when I first sit down to plan and start a new book chapter, this is the most vulnerable time for me when I'm most susceptible to procrastination. The first thing is to be aware of the fact and own it. Next is a play; I give myself an hour, which I time with a countdown timer, and I listen to music that nurtures my creativity, mostly meditation music. My favorite choice for this is anything from Sonic Yogi. It helps me to get in the zone. And lastly, to have a due date, such that if you don't meet it you will be letting someone else down. This helps me to be gentle with myself and to manage procrastination so that it doesn't manage me.

*Substitution: Transforming well-worn patterns of behavior doesn't always happen overnight. Sometimes we need to ween ourselves off what is not working for us and move into our ideal set of circumstances and way of living. Substituting ginger beer for beer isn't necessarily the healthiest choice, either, but ginger beer is healthier than beer, and it doesn't come with the side effects of beer. Of course, it's a personal choice, and only you know what you really need to let go of so that you can move forward with your life. I also used to drink way too much wine. It wasn't really adding value to my life, so I substituted tea for wine, and now I consider myself a bit of a tea connoisseur. It's a whole other world, and the various kinds of teas that are available are enormous. My favorite teas come from Vietnam and China. They are so good and healthy for you, as well as rich in antioxidants. It was the perfect substitution for me.

***Creating a vision:** This enables you to step into the person you wish to become and to transform your self-perception of who you think you are and what you are capable of achieving in life. Creating a vision for my life has helped me to take on projects that would be impossible to achieve without one. Having a vision increases the chances of you meeting that vision with success. And as you embody your vision, it starts to pull you along. The synchronicities that show up will blow your mind. The synergy I have with the universe and the movie documentary that I created and produced has been amazing. I needed to attract an advisor, and one showed up. I needed a director, and one showed up. I needed to attract a screen writer, and one showed up. It's been an amazing roller coaster ride and an adventure of a lifetime. Create a positive vision that scares you and allow yourself to be taken along for the ride. Then watch your life and self-imagine transform right before your eyes.

***Developing courage:** At some point, if transformation is going to occur, we need to face our fears. Fear of change, fear of making a mistake, fear of failure, fear of success, and the list goes on and on. Through facing that which we fear, we can transform that fear into courage, and courage is what is needed to show up and to create momentum and positive changes for our lives. It takes courage to make a decision to change and to let go of what is no longer serving you and to make choices that empower you to live your life to your full potential. Doing something outside your comfort zone on a regular basis will help you to the develop your courage muscle. One of the things that has been really beneficial for me is getting involved with Toastmasters International in Bali. It has helped me to practice public speaking on a regular basis and has increased my flying hours. I also mentor and help other members to increase their confidence in speaking English in front of groups. I find it rewarding to reach back and to lift other people up. It's great to be able to support and encourage other people to step outside their comfort zones. Public speaking is one of the skills that never goes out of fashion, and the nerves never really go away. You just have to give them a different meaning, changing that feeling from fear to one of excitement. There isn't really much difference between the two. The main difference is your expectation of the end result. When it's your birthday, you normally get excited—right?—because you are expecting good things to come your way. It's the same with public speaking and building courage. I expect the best outcome for myself and I've put in a lot of hours to get this result. Therefore I'm excited to do presentations.

I encourage you to do a transformation list like mine below so that you can reflect on your life and see how far you have come and can see the potential that you are capable of demonstrating in your life.

You might surprise yourself.

I Transformed:

- from not knowing how to read and write at a basic level until I was ten, to now coaching and encouraging others to write for the first time.

- from being terrified of public speaking to now delivering presentations around the world.

- from a career in landscaping to becoming a writer, publisher, producer, life-coach, and NLP trainer.

- from not having travelled overseas to now having traveled to every contingent except Antarctica.

- from self-medicating with drugs to living a healthy lifestyle.

- from not knowing anything about publishing to now being considered an expert.

- from never volunteering my time to now consistently giving my time away to help others for free.

- from never giving to charity to donating the proceeds of the *A Journey of Riches* book launches to charity (The proceeds of this book will go to the Bali Street Kids Foundation, which helps to keep orphan children off the streets and putting them into good homes.)

- from not having a high opinion of myself to now being a man with grounded confidence, and I don't care what other people think of me.

I'll leave you with this quote that I discovered. Hopefully you can glean something from it.

"Change is inevitable but transformation is by conscious choice."

~ Heather Ash Amara

"You and I possess within ourselves - at every moment of our lives, under all circumstances, the power to transform the quality of our lives. Knowing that is what the work is all about."

~ Werner Erhard

CHAPTER 3

Transform Your Mind

By Alexander Hoffmann

My journey through life has been filled with richness since I can remember. I was born in Venezuela, South America, to a blessed middle-class family of six. I'm the youngest of four, and my parents have always been hard working people and self-made entrepreneurs.

My dad was born in Austria from hard-working parents who experienced World War II in their own flesh. After many struggles from war, they migrated to Brazil in South America looking for a fresh new start. The ship got broken in the middle of the sea and they were sent to Venezuela, and that's how I ended up being a Venezuelan. My mom grew up with a single mom and was fortune enough to go to the United States of America and experience the new world at a young age.

My life has been filled with richness in every sense of the word. Since I can remember, I have experienced traveling the world, meeting important people, helping the less fortune during natural disasters, serving as a missionary in some of the poorest places of Latin America, and eating some of the wildest food in the world while sitting in the floor. From studying in one of the best business schools of the world and reaching the highest titles and salaries of private enterprises, my professional life has been filled with many opportunities to enrich the lives of thousands of people around the world. I have been blessed with five amazing kids that transform my life on a daily basis and are my greatest joy and my best teachers.

When John Spender reached out to me about writing this chapter and talked about the subject *"Transformation Calling,"* I was going through one of my biggest transformations of my 46 years of life. After having gone through my own *journey of riches*, I had to make a long stop and redesign my life all over. Thanks to the great life that I briefly described before, when I started my transformation process, I had accumulated the tools and experiences that I needed in order to survive all of the difficulties that I faced. I believe that everybody has deep within themselves the tools to overcome any challenge in life. Within this chapter, I will share with you some of the tools that I used during my transformation, and how everything starts with the mind.

"The more obstacles you face and overcome, the more times you falter and get back on track, the more difficulties you struggle with and conquer, the more resiliency you will naturally develop. There is nothing that can hold you back, if you are resilient."

~ Jim Rohn

I Nourish my Mind Daily

Just like the physical body needs balancing and nutritious food to have good health, the mind also needs nutritious and healthy thoughts in order to have a creative space. In order to exchange old limiting beliefs with new empowering beliefs, I needed to write new information. The subconscious mind is like a hard drive that has several disks with information and the only way to change that information is by writing new information on top of the old. Unfortunately we don't have a delete button to get rid of the bad information or experiences of life. So, I always surround myself with positive people and read good books. They help me nurture my mind so that I can write positive information into the subconscious mind. Affirmations also help me rewrite new empowering information into my mind, and so I speak them daily.

"Nourish the mind like you would your body. The mind cannot survive on junk food."

~ Jim Rohn

I Detox my Mind Daily

Toxic thoughts are as limiting and destructive as the plague. I always take care of myself and escape from any toxic situation, thoughts, and even people, as if it were a contagious disease. As the old saying goes, "One bad apple spoils the whole barrel," depending on the length of time that it's left there. There are rotten apples all over the place, and you are the only one responsible for identifying them and removing them from your life quickly. I always surround myself with people who are on the way to where I want to be.

"You are the sum of the five people you spend the most time with. Choose wisely."

~ Jim Rohn

Toxic thoughts limit you because they block the flow of energy and new ideas to the mind, and you want to make sure your imagination is always vibrant. Imagination is the main source of all creativity and the creation of new ideas and new opportunities in life. People with toxic thoughts get sick more often than others and have a lower level of energy and creativity, and as a consequence they are stuck in life. Discovering negative thoughts, neutralizing them, and replacing them with positive thoughts that empower you to achieve more is a daily task. In my own experience, it is more difficult to achieve this level of consciousness when you are in the middle of a crisis.

Being aware of what I say and think is a habit I have developed in order to overcome challenges. The best way to determine my thoughts is through my words. I started being aware of what I say, when I say it, and how I say it. I do a daily self-analysis of the thoughts in my subconscious mind that are limiting my beliefs and convert them into empowering beliefs.

Exercise and Creativity

> "Imagination is more important than knowledge. For knowledge is limited, whereas imagination embraces the entire world, stimulating progress, giving birth to evolution."
>
> ~ Albert Einstein

Imagination is the precursor of creativity. Imagination allows you to dream of all the things that are impossible for the rational mind, and creativity gives you the ideas to make it a reality in your own life. My best moments of creativity have been while I'm having some type of intense physical activity. At that moment the mind leaves aside the concerns of the past and connects with the possibilities of the present and the future. When I change my physical state, my body produces chemicals that put me in a positive state of mind and ignite the creativity and creation of new thoughts, new ways of doing things.

One of the reasons I exercise every day is because I have found a source of creativity and strength in my mind and body through the production of endorphins. Endorphins are chemicals that produce a state of wellness and joy in our bodies. They stimulate parts of the brain that bring feelings of happiness and relieve pain and discomfort from the body and cause a feeling of vitality.

Set the Right Actors in your Play

The mind is like a scenario in which a play is presented every day. I create it with all the information I have in my subconscious mind, plus all the information that I obtain from my daily experiences. I have the power to allow actors to enter or exit the play. Remember that you are the director of your play. If the actors and the script are positive, then the play is positive. If the play has a horror theme, then the results will be of horror.

Remember that the mind processes information. If I give negative input, it is going to create a negative output. If I give positive and empowering thoughts, the outcome will be positive and great. My daily routine is to nurture my mind and put it in a stage of positive scenes. Celebrate life and all the blessings that you have. Become a caretaker of your thoughts and eliminate the negatives and limiting beliefs so that you can make space for the positive and empowering thoughts.

My Words Shape my World

The spoken word has power and I have learned that my personal power comes from the words I say on a daily basis. The thoughts we have and the words that we speak constantly are creating our present and our future. Unfortunately the education system does not teach us the effect that emotions have on words, nor how words affect the emotions, depending on how the words are said.

Our beliefs shape our lives, and the things we say are an extension of our thoughts. The best way to change my life is by changing my thoughts. This is perhaps one of the most revolutionary thoughts of the last couple of decades. Only by changing our thoughts and our words can we change everything that is around us.

"If you want to be responsible for your life, you have to be responsible for your mouth."

~ Louise L. Hay

Our words are orders for the brain and we must understand that the brain cannot differentiate between what is a joke and what is serious. This is one of the reasons why I became more aware and took care of things that I say. When we say something negative, we produce a toxic state that passes to some people who might identify with that expression and take it as their own and believe that they have already become that person, such as "I am very anxious" or "I am too dumb" or "I cannot afford that." All of these are judgments that I have heard and repeated myself. The more I repeated them unconsciously, the more I have come to believe them and think that I am that kind of person. Now, understand that everything was created through the use of language. Just as I've created this negative reality with the language I used, I can also rewrite something positive through the power of affirmations. Experts call it retraining the mind or re-recording the information into the subconscious mind.

"We are what we do every day. So excellence is not an act, but a habit."

~ Aristotle

The Power of Beliefs

"What we can or can't do, what we consider possible or impossible, is rarely based on our true capacity, but rather it is a function of our beliefs about who we are."

~ Anthony Robbins

We normally plan according to our beliefs, and our behavior is generated from a belief system. Our brain considers beliefs and realities as truths, and the only way to change them is through affirmations. For example, our relationship with money has to do with the beliefs that are stored in our subconscious minds from childhood. We can create superficial stories of our dreams, but if there is a shadow of a doubt, it will stop us from what we really want. The confidence that makes me feel comfortable comes from the belief that I am capable of more.

We all have a belief system that is like a map, and it is the force that guides us every day in the thoughts and actions we take. This belief system creates my behavior and it is what has led me to achieve what I have or do not have. In other words, my belief system creates my reality. If I have not achieved what I want, then I need to start working in my belief system. My belief system gives me an emotional certainty when my capabilities are attacked.

Belief in Yourself

"You have something special. You have greatness within you."

~ Les Brown

This is the most important of all beliefs, and the one that I had to give my best personal effort. I have invested time and money to train myself to become a better person and a better leader. It requires a lot of daily effort, and it's something I can learn and master if I want to become a transformational leader. As mentioned before, it all begins in the mind.

There are limiting beliefs and empowering beliefs. The limiting beliefs are those that disable us from thinking and acting in a determined way during a specific situation. Empowering beliefs help us to improve our self-esteem and our confidence because they enhance our capabilities, giving us security to face daily challenges. Again I repeat this important principle; this is a daily task that we face. Our subconscious minds will always direct us immediately to our most primitive ways of thinking, which we have to discover for ourselves. And it's only through affirmations that I have reprogrammed my most powerful computer, my mind.

People will follow you only if you are congruent with what you say you are going to do. A consistent leader builds confidence with his actions not only with his words. Believing in yourself is the first step toward transformation. Believe that you can achieve everything you can dream of.

"When your words and actions match, people know they can trust you."

~ John C. Maxwell

I am the Architect of My Future

If you want things to change for you, you have to change yourself first. If you want things to improve for you, you have to improve yourself first. The mind is like a muscle, and all the actions that you generate physically are created in your mind first. You are the architect of your life and you create your own reality. Your mind has the power to create it all or destroy it all. Every day that goes by in your life, you are either growing or dying through each of your thoughts and interactions with the world. Understand that your beliefs are the roots where your destiny is created.

"Your beliefs become your thoughts,
Your thoughts become your words,
Your words become your actions,
Your actions become your habits,
Your habits become your values,
Your values become your destiny."

~ Gandhi

Begin with an End in Mind and you will Make it.

"Begin with an End in Mind" is based on the principle that all things are created twice. To everything there is a mental creation first and a physical creation second. Stephen R. Covey, one of my mentors and author of the book *The 7*

Habits of Highly Effective People, taught me this principle many years ago. I was the president of the Brigham Young University's Alumni Association, and I had the opportunity to host him in a conference in Mexico City. During the seminar, he taught me this valuable principle of "Begin with an End in Mind" and the different implications it could have in my personal and professional life if I apply it on a daily basis. From that moment on, my life changed for the better. I started creating a different reality in my life by beginning with an end in mind.

I create my own reality every day from what I create in my mind. It is so simple and at the same time a little bit complicated. Remember the dreams you stopped believing. Maybe someone told you that it was not for you or that the dreams were not possible. If you allowed someone to destroy that dream in your mind, now is the time to begin with a new end in mind. The mind is the beginning of any physical creation. So, if you create it mentally first, you can make it a reality in your life.

"Begin with an End in Mind" helps me develop a clear vision which will give me the stability I need to drive my business toward my goals. A good architect designs a blueprint and then builds. The blueprint gives me not only the basis of the outcome, and how to create the structure of my life, but it will also keep me focused during the journey.

Cleanse my Mind Through Meditation

"You should sit in meditation for 20 minutes a day, unless you are too busy; then you should sit for an hour."

~ Old Zen Saying.

Why Meditation? Because some questions cannot be answered by Google. When I quiet my mind, the soul speaks to me. Meditation helps me discover the answer that is deep inside of me and which I need for a specific moment in my life. Meditation is a great tool to put my mind into a state of conscious rest in which I stop all the external flow of information and have a connection with my inner soul. Meditation cleanses my mind just like fasting cleanses my body.

Many cultures do a monthly fast to cleanse the body of toxins. It also works with the mind. The fasting of the mind is meditation. It is the best tool to pause the excessive flow of external information into the mind and put the past and the future aside and only focus on the present. Stop thinking of external factors and focus on internal soul-searching. Meditation is a disconnection of distracting external impulses and will help you detoxify your mind and give you space so you can get new thoughts, new ideas, and a new life. Remember that creativity is the mother of all inventions and the clearer your mind is, the more creativity you will be able to reach. You cannot create or invent any new ideas with a toxic mind.

"The worst enemy to creativity is self doubt."

~ Sylvia Plath

I Have a Dream!

During a recent trip to Washington DC, I went to the Lincoln Memorial and stood right where Martin Luther King pronounced his famous speech, "I Have a Dream." Back in 1963, he was able to gather 250,000 people without the power of social media, just because he had a dream, and, interestingly enough, his dream changed the world.

A clear and determined vision begins with a big dream. No great achievement comes without dreams. Never let anyone make you think that your dreams are too insignificant to achieve or that you cannot accomplish them. It was never assumed that they would be easy; if they were, they wouldn't be dreams. Keep your vision in the right focus and make your dreams the center of your vision. The bigger the dream, the clearer the vision is going to be.

"I think if you are an entrepreneur, you've got to dream big and then dream bigger."

~ Howard Schultz

Someone is Waiting for You!

"A leader is one who sees more than others see, who sees farther than others see, and who sees before others see."

~ Leroy Eimes

Everybody faces problems, and successful people face more problems than others, because they try more things and try harder until they accomplish their goals. Sometimes mistakes provide opportunities for growth and have taught me how to get back on my feet. The wisdom and experience accumulated throughout the years gives me the ability to anticipate the difficulties faced in the near future. It's the same with an airplane pilot: the more hours of experience, the better she is to face the storms.

A great leader is always looking beyond the difficulties to tell you where you need to go and what you must know to get where you want to be. I always teach my people not to listen to the unbelieving critics and also to be careful with the seeds of doubt. I train them so they are not overwhelmed by the challenges. I encourage them to look for simple solutions, and always instill confidence in them. I love this quote from a great leader:

"Doubt your doubts, but never doubt your beliefs."

~ Dieter F. Utchdorf.

A great leader spends all the time needed asking as many questions as possible to identify the needs of others. This is the only way that I can guide others. Taking the title of a leader has a lot of responsibilities and it takes a lot of heart to guide people to their dreams. It's not an easy task, but you can learn it with time and experience, and by developing a sincere interest in others.

"A leader with a clear vision informs the way his followers should follow, and guides them through the difficulties and meets their needs on the road ahead."

~ Simon Sinek

Leaders Add Value to Others

I only follow leaders that inspire me, not only because of what they have accomplished, but also because of who they have become. A leader who inspires is willing to constantly add value to his followers. That was one of the first lessons I learned from one of my mentors and coaches, John C. Maxwell. When I first met him, he kept repeating this phrase all the time: "Leaders add value to others." After repeating this principle many times, I understood two things: the first one is that, if I did not add value in every interaction with my followers, my leadership was weakening. And second is that the best way to add value to people was by inspiring them to be better people and to look for more achievements in their lives. That is one of the first and most important responsibilities of a leader. My people need my constant words of encouragement. They need to know that I believe in them and that I am here to help them overcome any difficult situation they are going to face.

"You never know when a moment and a few sincere words can have an impact on a life."

~ Zig Ziglar

Everybody is watching what you are doing, and people like to follow positive and enthusiastic leaders. Nobody likes to follow negative or pessimistic leaders, at least not in my life. Are you a magnet that attracts people with the same virtues to be positive and enthusiastic? If not, you need to start adding value to people every day until you can master it.

What Drives you?

A leader with true passion connects with the heart and ignites the hidden emotions that have been turned off in the traditional automated world. When the real needs of my people are clear, then I can lead them to an emotional state that will generate the type of passion they need on a daily basis to overcome all the obstacles in life. Passion is the emotion that leads me to action and inspires me with a clear vision to pursue my dreams, no matter how many obstacles I find in my way.

Passion comes from the heart, which is the center of all emotions. Passion is the deep love that moves the disappointed and the discouraged people to the hopeful state of achieving their dreams. Passion is an emotion that moves everyone to achieve things that were not possible before under different and difficult circumstances. Passion ignites an invisible force that is in all of us and is the most powerful spark that can light a massive crowd of people. A person with passion generates the energy to keep himself going even during the most difficult times of life.

"The Heart is more powerful than the brain. The heart is about 60 times stronger electrically and up to 5,000 times stronger magnetically than the brain."

~ Heartmath.org

Be Humble

One of the complexities people are facing in this materialistic life is pride. I heard a great leader say many times, "In order to be a great leader you need to swallow your pride." There is no space for ego. In order to be your best self, the most important person is the person you are serving. You need to make sure you are always willing to serve, to listen, and to humble yourself in order to understand the needs of the other person. That will accelerate the speed of trust and you will be able to help other people achieve their dreams faster.

> "Humility is required to seek feedback. It requires wisdom to understand it, analyze it, and act on it properly."
>
> ~ Stephen R. Covey

When I understand that it is not about me anymore, but about how I can help others achieve their dreams, then I become my best self. It's not about how much money I make. It's not about how much I know. It's not about how much recognition I have received. It's not about how much I have traveled the world. It's about how many lives I have impacted and how many people I have served in my life.

Be my Best Self

"You must take personal responsibility. You cannot change the circumstances, the seasons, or the wind, but you can change yourself. That is something you have charge of."

~ Jim Rohn

"Be my best self" doesn't mean only personal growth. "Be my best self" is based on the concept that humans only use less than 10% of their maximum capacities. That includes the brain, the emotions, the body, the spirit, and all the resources that I have been given. A large number of people go through this life mainly because they want to become a better person in order to fulfill their dreams. Today I tell you, be your best self. Don't settle for what you have; you can do more, and you can have 10 times more. You are probably not running at your maximum potential.

The quality and level of experiences obtained in my life have quickly broken paradigms and given me a quantum leap forward unlike anything else. There is no other moment in life where personal development plays such an important roll in the success of your life. A rich person is better known for who he or she becomes and not only for the material things s/he acquires.

I bless you to live *A Journey of Riches* and to find your *Transformation Calling*.

"I know this transformation is painful, but you're not falling apart; you're just falling into something different, with a new capacity to be beautiful."

~ William C. Hannan

CHAPTER 4

Something Magical Is Happening

By Katie Neubaum

I am a lover of life, a dreamer, and a rainbow chaser. I believe in miracles and in all things magical. I live to connect and contribute something meaningful and powerful in this lifetime.

I am from Columbia, South Carolina. I was raised here and grew up in a loving family with four siblings: Ken, Melinda, Christy and Rosemary. I loved my childhood. My mother Linda was a beauty queen full of laughter and song. She was always singing and dancing with us. She taught me to love more, give more and be more. My father was a champion swimming competitor, a musician, and businessman. He was at every athletic and musical event, and he is the one responsible for instilling persistence and positivity into my character. As a family we enjoyed lots of camping, boating, biking and hiking. We were raised in the Church of Jesus Christ of Latter Day Saints, perhaps better known as Mormons. We woke up as a family at 6am, and then those of us who were in high school also attended morning seminary before school. Every Sunday we went to church, adhered to church standards, and sought to be righteous and charitable.

As a young girl I was very interested in music. I loved to sing and play the piano. I would jump at any opportunity to perform. I loved the attention and the glamour of the costumes and the big stage. I started taking classical voice lessons when I was 13. I remember my teacher saying, "Wow, you have a big voice! You will be a famous opera singer!" I believed her and I wanted that more than anything else. I attended lessons weekly and I practiced every day. In high school I auditioned for every talent show and competition in town. When I was a junior, I auditioned for the Governor's School of Performing Arts. This was a prestigious summer program for talented musicians. The competition was tough and the slots available were very limited. I was honored to have been chosen as a scholarship recipient to attend the five week program. The following Summer I attended Brevard Music School in North Carolina. This was the first time I had really been exposed to the opera world. It was exhilarating and now I knew it was happening!

The following school year my father accepted a job in Florida. I will never forget arriving in Florida and noticing all of the manicured highways. There were palm trees and beautiful gardens all along the way. South Carolina is a beautiful state, but it does not compare to the blue skies, thick, green grass and sandy, white beaches of South Florida. We loved the weather, the people and all the opportunities available there. I learned a lot through that experience. I was not happy that I had to leave before my senior year but knew it was a necessary move for our family. I found it easier to flow with the direction my life was taking and see that my father's decision could be a window of opportunity for me.

Throughout my senior year, I was auditioning for music scholarships. Being a Mormon, I really wanted to attend Brigham Young University in either Utah or Idaho. I always thought it would be easier to attend college with others who shared my same religious beliefs. The audition went very well and I received a full vocal scholarship to the branch in Idaho. I was elated! I finished up at Marjory Stoneman Douglas High school and started preparing for my adventures out West.

After I graduated, I decided to take a trip to Europe to visit a young man named Pieter whom I had met in Governor's school. I was there for music and he was there with a basketball team from Belgium. Pieter and I had a sweet relationship that felt more like a fairytale to me. The entire experience with him was an unexpected romantic adventure. We had a fun love crush that summer, and we kept in touch via snail mail and occasional long distance calls over the course of the next year. I had always dreamed of visiting foreign lands and I loved the idea of flying on an airplane across the seas. I worked a part-time job in high school and saved enough money to make it happen. I flew into Brussels, Belgium. Pieter and his family met me there and took me back to their home. I loved how each window on the front and back of the house had fresh flowers growing in flower boxes. I loved the skinny streets and tiny, fast cars. I loved hearing the French and Dutch languages all around me. I loved late-night pancakes and beer. Their home was in Kortrijk, Belgium and we would soon head to the coast to a beach town called Oostende. From there, we headed out to see Paris, France! Oh my goodness, I thought I was in heaven! I had only dreamed of seeing Paris. This magical experience taught me that everything is possible! I desired it greatly. I planned out every detail in my mind of how it would feel to be in Europe. I imagined the people I would meet and the places I would go. I learned that my imagination coupled with my unyielding desire and determination would make everything possible!

Now it was off to college at BYU, Idaho! I arrived and the excitement began! I was free and on my own. I was in a dorm room with five other freshmen girls and I was registered for 18 credit hours and ready to hit the ground running. Classes and Choir began and it was all very new and exciting! It was amazing to share my first college experience with others who shared my religious beliefs and values. It was good until winter hit and the sidewalks became ice. I was miserable! I decided to go back to Florida and find a local college to attend. The Florida sun was glorious! It was so good to be home. I started working a part-time job as a singing waitress at Ramano's Macaroni Grill. I thought that would be fun until I knew where I was going to go to continue my education. I loved it and the crowd loved me. It actually served as a great training ground for my singing, and the money was excellent too.

During one of my Macaroni Grill performances, the opera director of the Florida Gold Coast opera heard me singing. He called me over to his table and said that 'although I didn't know it, I had just inadvertently auditioned for a part in his next opera'! I was very excited, though it ended up being a part in the chorus. The opera chorus was a great way to learn. To my surprise, the director liked me so much that he referred me to audition for a scholarship for voice lessons at the University of Miami. I was flattered and honored to have the chance to study at such a well-known music school. I rehearsed with the opera director for a few days to prepare and off I went. The Voice teacher's name was Joseph Evans. He had an extensive background in music and performing. I was nervous to sing for him but knew that I had to give it my all. I decided to sing a simple aria from the *24 Italian songbook* called *Vittoria Mio Core*. I had great success with this one before and I enjoyed singing it. I closed my eyes and took a deep breath. I nodded to the accompanist and he began to play. My voice was warm and vibrant and it flowed just as I hoped it would. I finished the aria and he smiled at me and said, "Your voice is beautiful Katie. I would be delighted to teach you." The feeling I had inside was like gumdrops and rainbows. I had gotten the scholarship to study with one of the greatest instructors at the Foster School of Music. Little did I know that he was preparing me for an even bigger audition to compete for a full scholarship to the University of Miami School of Music. I had about two months to prepare for it. I was driven and determined to receive the scholarship, as I knew that Miami was a private university and that it would be the only way that I would be able to afford to attend. I worked hard and prepared to the best of my ability and I nailed the audition. Within about a week I received a phone call informing me that I was one of the top recipients and was being offered a full scholarship to attend the University of Miami as a Vocal Performance Major. It was one of the most exciting times in my life. My experience studying there and working with first class teachers and students was pure bliss. I realized throughout my studies that I could accomplish great things. I experienced a lot of growing pains along the way and had to get used to standing in my power as I was learning to be a responsible adult. Growing up, I depended on my parents a lot, maybe even too much. They were always there to clean up my messes and wipe my tears. I was grateful for the positive mindset that my father had influenced us all to have. He challenged me throughout my childhood to never ever quit.

In the summer of my junior year at Miami, there was an opportunity affiliated with the university to attend a Summer Music Academy in Austria. I had never been to Austria and the thought of it excited me greatly! There were five half scholarships and five full scholarships granted. I auditioned and was awarded one of the full scholarships. I was stoked! I finished up the year at Miami and then headed to Austria for five weeks to study music and learn the German language. I was housed with a local family and attended class every day. I also attended operas, workshops, master classes and scheduled tours to see the country and enjoy the beautiful Austrian culture. It was a splendid experience that I reflect upon often.

Upon graduating I returned home to South Carolina. I was offered to stay at Miami and complete my graduate studies, but in my heart I wanted to be married and start a family. Many of my friends stayed to continue their education. That did not appeal to me. I had dreams of being a great mother and having a big family like my mom did. So the decision was made and I returned home.

In the Mormon religion it is highly recommend that we only date and marry someone of our same faith. I had been living the standards of the church my entire life and I truly believed in eternal marriage, and I wanted more than anything to marry a righteous man Who was worthy of marrying me in the Lord's house, the holy temple of the Church of Jesus Christ of Latter Day Saints. I began attending the young single adult events and I went to church every Sunday with them too. Within a few weeks of being home I met a young man by the name of Dave. He was tall, dark and handsome. Most of all, he was funny! He made me laugh hard and I love to laugh. He was a military police officer in the United States Army. He would come to the Wednesday night scripture study in his uniform and I was always excited to see him. Eventually, he asked me out and we had a blast. We began to date regularly and quickly fell madly in love. Shortly after we were engaged and then married. We had a beautiful temple marriage in addition to a civil ceremony to ensure that our non-Mormon friends and family could enjoy the celebration as well.

Dave and I were married for about a year when I decided to join the Army too. I had always admired the service men and women. My Grandfather and Grandmother Berner also served in the military, and their stories were fascinating to me. I felt an obligation and a great desire to serve, so I did. I went through the entire process and got to the point of choosing what would be my field of expertise throughout my service. I was not sure what to choose. Luckily, the recruiters knew how to guide me. They told me that I tested high on the Army aptitude test and that they recommended that I choose Military Intelligence. I was baffled! I am a musician and math is my weakest subject. The recruiter explained to me that it was the best deal for me. There was a big bonus of $12,000 attached to that job and my first duty station would be Hawaii. I was sold and I swore in on January 19th, 2000 and headed off to nine weeks of boot camp in

Fort Leonard Wood, Missouri. When I arrived it was cold. I get along with almost everyone, but here on day zero, as they called it, we were not even allowed to smile. Everyone looked the same. Plain faces, camouflage uniforms, black combat boots and a hat. I was used to being the star of the show, and now I was nobody. I was Specialist West. I had no make up or fancy perfume, I was just a number. I survived the gas chamber, weapons training, ruck marching, and I even passed the final PT test with a broken rib, a twisted ankle and bronchitis. I used duct tape to bandage myself up. There was no way I was going to be recycled and start boot camp over again.

Off to Schofield Barracks Hawaii I went! I felt proud and excited to have made it through. When I arrived in Hawaii, the locals were welcoming and the unit I was assigned to was great! I enjoyed learning the skills of Electronic Warfare and I loved being a part of a joint operations mission in the Kunia Regional Operations Center. The building we worked in was actually located underneath a pineapple field. Literally, the escape route for us was through a hatch that opened into a field of pineapples. The experience of becoming an Intelligence Analyst was remarkable. I learned to overcome obstacles with ease and how to lead others with confidence. The lessons I learned have presented themselves throughout my entire life. I am forever grateful that I made the choice to serve my country.

In the second year of my contract I was offered an apprentice sponsorship with the Hawaii Opera Theater. I was excited to be able to continue my singing as well. Shortly after the opera contract was offered I found out that I was pregnant with my first child, Andrew. Dave and I were ready to start our family so it was not a shock. We were thrilled!

My world was seemingly perfect and all of my dreams were coming true. Then the phone rang. It was about 6am in Hawaii and I was getting ready for PT with the unit. It was my mom and she was crying hysterically and told me to turn on the TV. I could not believe what I was seeing. I witnessed the second plane hitting the twin towers in New York City. It was terrifying! The unit called and alerted us that everyone was on lockdown and that the maximum security was in place. All units would be activated and our mission as intelligence analysts was about to get intense. My husband and all of our friends were likely going to war. It was a difficult time for our military and for our entire nation.

The war was in full action and work was busier than ever. It was March 28, 2002 and Andrew was born. He was a big, beautiful baby. There were a few complications with his delivery but all I remember is how much I adored the sunshine in his big brown eyes and his sweet temperament. Andrew is now almost 16 years old! He is 6'1", which is tall for his age, and quite large too. He is a lineman and has played on the Varsity team since he was a freshman. He has an excellent baritone singing voice and also plays the guitar, piano and violin. I am honored to call him mine and I am so grateful for all that he has taught me.

My four year term had ended, and it was time to make a decision about staying in the Army or moving on to my next adventure. I had also injured my back during combat training and was experiencing a lot of pain on a daily basis. Due to the war, we were on a Stop-Loss. This means no one could get out. I applied to get out because of my personal hardships. My back was giving me problems and I had just found out that Andrew needed to have a kidney surgery. I wanted to take him back to South Carolina to get the medical attention he needed while having the support of my family. Luckily, my request was granted. Dave and I also decided to divorce and go our separate ways. We had grown apart throughout the war and mutually felt that divorce was in order. We got a quick divorce and have remained wonderful friends and have co-parented Andrew joyfully.

When we were settled back in South Carolina and had successfully completed the surgery, I returned to college to obtain my graduate degree in Vocal Performance and Music Education. During this time I remarried, had my son Joseph, and 20 months later I had Victoria. My second husband and I had a very volatile relationship from the beginning. He had a hard time adjusting to being Andrew's stepfather and we realized quickly that we were not compatible. We stayed together for 10 years and tried to make it work but there was no way. We argued a lot and we struggled financially too. I had become terribly overweight and depressed. As a last ditch effort to save our marriage John joined the Army and headed off to Officer's Candidate School. We thought that perhaps a better income and a little separation would help. I suppose it helped in some ways, but in other ways it was tragic. I had no one to help me with the three children and I was extremely unhealthy and tired all the time.

One day, while the children were sleeping, I went out into the hot sun to do yard work and I felt a sharp pain in the back of my head. I went inside to get some water and immediately started having a severe migraine. This migraine lasted seven days and nothing made it subside. I decided to go to the doctor and was referred to the hospital. The doctor ordered a cat scan and found that I had had a mini stroke and that's what was causing my intense head pain. I was in the hospital for a week and they did every test possible and were unable to discover the cause. They deemed it as stress-related and put me on bed rest and pain medicine. This is when I knew I had to find a solution for weight loss and my overall well-being. I joined a gym and started dieting. I started a new diet about every three weeks. Nothing was working, and now I was in self-sabotaging mode. I was sneaking fast food meals frequently and justifying it because I was having a bad day or because I didn't have time to cook. To make matters worse, late at night when my husband and children were sleeping, I would quietly creep into the kitchen to eat. There was a place between my refrigerator and my counter tops that I could squeeze my large behind into. I would squish into my happy place with my diet soda and eat an entire row of Oreos and half a bag of Doritos.

Sometimes I would watch recorded soap operas while I ate, but usually I would eat so quickly while I hid, to avoid anyone seeing what I was actually eating. When I would wake up the next day after binging, my body was bloated and swollen from all the sodium and preservatives. I felt like I had hit rock bottom and maybe I should just drive off a bridge and end my misery. I was no one. I was so exhausted. I felt like a dead woman walking most of the time. At that point, I weighed 255 pounds and was a size 22-24, which was the largest size available in my favorite plus size stores. I knew there was no size up for me to grow into. I was embarrassed thinking about the possibility of there not being clothes big enough to fit me. I was ashamed to go to events or even to my children's school. I had not been overweight my entire life. I always had a larger, muscular build and broad shoulders, but I was also an athlete throughout my life. I ran track, and played softball, basketball, volleyball, and was even a cheerleader. I loved working out, and I desired more than anything to get this extra weight off of my body. I could barely walk without getting out of breath so I didn't exercise much. Also, it was humiliating to feel like I was one of the fattest people in the gym.

I decided to stop trying to diet and looked into having gastric bypass surgery. I went through the entire process of learning, meeting with a psychiatrist and scheduling my procedure with the surgeon. I really hated that I was going to have most of my stomach removed but I just couldn't live one more year with this awful obese body! The surgery was scheduled. I had a plan.

While I was working out one day, I overheard a couple of gym members talking about a new program that they were having success with. I had the surgery scheduled, but maybe I could get off a few pounds before the surgery and start the process of losing weight. A few days later, my friend Jennifer Trinkner from the gym called me to tell me about her experience with the Isagenix program. She told me that it was not a diet, rather a cellular cleanse and fat burning system. She explained that there was a 100% money back guarantee and that I could enter the IsaBody Challenge for a chance to win $25,000! I even became hopeful about the small possibility that it might just work so well that I could cancel my surgery. I was hopeful and I was looking forward to see and feel my results.

My big brown box of products arrived just two days later. Little did I know that November 12, 2012 would be the day that my entire life would change. I opened the box and planned to execute this 30 day program as if my life depended on it because...well...it actually did. The first day was a breeze. I was satisfied with the taste of the protein shakes and I was able to calculate my calories and resist my late-night binge eating ceremony. I call it that because it had become a daily activity that I looked forward to more than anything else. It was a ritual...my time to unwind and feed my depression so that I could feel better if only for a little while.

Food had become my friend and the object of my affection. I turned to food for comfort and security. The next couple of days were also pretty easy. The only thing I was truly missing was my diet soda. I used to drink that instead of water. It was the one item that I believed was good for me, so I didn't understand why I could not have it. The week was coming to an end and it was time for my very first 24-hour cellular cleanse day. I was dreading it all day and did not think I would make it through. I mean, how would a food addict like me not eat for 24 hours and only drink beverages and eat a couple of little round snacks designed to break up visceral fat and also keep me full? It was pretty scary to imagine, but I had made a promise to myself to give it 100% effort.

Sunday was cleanse day and it had arrived. I woke up full of anxiety but also full of hope. The first cleanse went down easily and I felt okay. I missed chewing food but I was not hungry at all. I drank all the scheduled beverages and ate the tiny snacks and I consumed about a gallon of water. I planned to go to bed early so that I would not be tempted to have my late night rendezvous with Oreos and Doritos. Luckily, I felt very tired and was able to get into the most unbelievably deep sleep. I woke up rested and full of energy! I felt happy and light. I felt an amazing amount of energy, and the inches also seemed to be dropping too. I continued on the 30-day program and could not believe the amount of weight that was dropping off. I released over 25 pounds in that first month. It was looking like I was going to be able to cancel my bariatric surgery after all. Because things were going so well, I decided to order another 30-day program.

My friends and family were curious about what I was doing, but I was not quite ready to go public with what I was doing. I planned to attend an event in January, 2013 to learn more about the integrity of the company as well as more about how I could possibly inspire others to become healthier too. When I arrived in Phoenix, Arizona at the Isagenix conference, I was amazed to see how many people were there. I was inspired by all of the stories, and charmed by the integrity and charisma of the owners of the company. As I watched and listened, a fire of hope started burning in my chest. I could see myself walking across the giant stage to receive accolades for sharing the very products that were making me feel so good. I had been using the products at that point for about two months and had released over 40 pounds. I had not had very much experience in sales, but I knew that I was a great communicator and that it should be easy enough to tell my story to others. I made a decision at that event to strive to better understand the industry of network marketing and to pursue building my own business with Isagenix. I was fired up and excited about the possibility of making it big! My friends and family soon caught the fever, and they were also experiencing rapid weight loss and energy increase. My business had become exciting! I was ready to take it to the next level. Before I knew it, I had dropped 85 pounds in that first year and was feeling and looking better than ever. I coached my new associates to attend the events with me and to share their stories too. In April of 2014, I had my first five figure month. I had quadrupled my income as a voice and piano teacher! The formula to success with this company was simple: eat the food, share the food, and repeat. Anyone could do this!

I was running one day in my neighborhood and I was thinking about how amazing my body was feeling and my business was thriving; but the one part of my life that was not working was my marriage. John and I had grown apart and he was really struggling with anger and violence in our home. I thought that if I could replace his income too, then I could afford to file for divorce and rid our home of violence once and for all. I came up with the idea to start coaching my teammates and other network marketers to leverage LinkedIn, a professional social media site, to create more free leads and make more money. I made an offer on our team page to individually coach clients for $150 for three sessions. Before I knew it, I had an eight week waiting list to coach with me. I was coaching for about six hours a day, and I was generating an additional $15,000 dollars per month. Soon after, I decided to create a three part webinar to serve the masses. I also wrote an eBook to go along with the course. This was also wildly successful! I was busier than ever and making more money than I ever dreamed possible!

Unfortunately, John and I were at the point of no return. We decided to make our separation official and begin the divorce proceedings. We stayed separated and our divorce was final a year later. Hitting the dating scene again was super intimidating. I had been out of the game for 11 years. Who would I find that wanted the responsibility of four people? It seemed like an impossible feat. I dated a couple of men and neither seemed like a long term fit. Then one day I was looking for a successful person on LinkedIn to interview live on my webinar when I came across a French opera singer named Yves. He agreed to do the interview with my attendees and me. During the interview, I realized that he was way more successful than I had imagined. He also had the ability to open doors for me to perform. He invited me to sing with him in Thailand the following month. Performing on the stages of the world was a part of my vision, and I was so excited to see it manifesting before my very eyes! That contract led to many other incredible opportunities. He was my agent, my duet partner and the object of my affection during that time. I performed in Thailand four times that year, then twice in Mexico, a few times on the East and West coast of USA and then in Paris, France. In the summer of 2017, I was in the middle of what would be my final performance for a while. I was in Las Vegas performing on my way to Thailand to perform for a couple of weeks, but my lower back pain had gotten so bad that it was uncomfortable to walk, sit, stand or even lie down. I decided to cancel my Asian singing tour and head home to get back surgery.

The surgery was greatly successful and I was healing like a champ! I had overcome my physical ailments and my bank account was flowing with abundance. I was thriving in Isagenix, LinkedIn coaching, performing, and mothering. Life was grand! The only thing missing now was my prince charming to make my fairytale a happily ever after one. Where would I meet someone who would love me and enjoy all the things that I adore? Who could be that special someone to see me for who I am and love my three children too?

I believe in the law of attraction and all the laws that govern the Universe. I made a list of all the qualities that I desired in a man. I called it my "Mary Poppins" list. Remember the scene in the movie where the children made a list of everything they wanted their new nanny to be? I decided to do the same thing. I made a very specific list. The way that I understand the law of attraction is that desires must be requested with absolute exactness, and with the feeling that you have already acquired that which you desire. I designed the man of my dreams and I began to visualize him throughout the day. Within about three days, my son Joey came into my room and told me that he had seen an advertisement on YouTube that showed a great dating site for singles over 40. I laughed and asked him why he was he telling me that. He told me that I seemed sad not having a boyfriend. He was certain that this dating site would help me find one. As adorable as it was, I ignored his idea and went on with my day.

Later that same afternoon I was working with my physical therapist. She and I were doing some stretches and she asked me if I had ever been on Tinder. This is the same exact site that my son had recommended. She continued to tell me how great the site was and that she had found all of her hot dates on there. I took this as a sign from the universe that the same site was mentioned in the same day. I set up my account and began to swipe. Within 30 minutes, I had over 50 swipes. (That means they liked my profile.) I was shocked and surprised but did not know exactly how to work it yet. In the next moment I received an instant message from a very good-looking guy named Joe. He had four pictures of himself but no description at all. It just said "Joe." His message said, "Hi." I replied, "Hi." He asked me how long I had been on Tinder and I replied, "30 Minutes." He found it amusing that he was the first one I had chatted with. We messaged back and forth and decided to have a drink the next day.

He drove to my city and we met at a nice bar. I was super nervous to meet him. When I arrived he was already there waiting for me in the parking lot. As I drove up I could see him. I parked my car and was even more nervous because he was even better looking in person. I got out of my car and there he was. He looked at me and smiled and kissed me right on the lips before he even said hello. I was blushing and giggling like a young schoolgirl. The drink at the bar turned into a bottle of wine and dinner. Joe and I hit it off from the second we connected. From that day we've been inseparable. We both felt as if we had known each other for many lifetimes. He was everything and more that I had requested from the universe. I joke and call him my "Mary Poppins Man!" It's been a little over four months since we met and the fireworks are still flying. We are aligned in all aspects of our lives and we are enjoying the romance and beauty of love and life. I suppose the next chapter of my story will reveal how this magical connection unfolds.

Transformation did call to me. I felt the calling from a deep place in my soul that was worthy of greatness! I longed to live a life of contribution and success. I desired to have childlike fun and enjoy every day to the fullest and that's what began to happen! The shift from being overweight, broke and depressed to happy, fit and financially free now seems like it was just a moment in time. I love my life so much. I love who I have become. I am excited to continue on this amazing journey. Whoever you are, I honor you for all that you are and all that you will become. Just remember that it begins with you and ends with you. You decide by your very thoughts what you will experience in this lifetime. I encourage you to choose the good thoughts and desires that serve you and bring you joy. Read good books, care for your body, and nurture your soul. Accept the calling to transform as I have. Set yourself free from the bondage of someone else's plan for you. You are worthy of all things great and magical.

"Just when the caterpillar
thought the world was over
it became a butterfly."

~ Zhuangzi

CHAPTER 5

Trusting the Voice of the Heart

By Noelani Love

We are currently at a pivotal time on our planet Earth; awakening as a collective humanity. I believe that we have existed on Earth in many previous lifetimes. But this time, we are here to do it right, so that we can achieve the next great golden age. Our planet is a being in and of itself, here for the purpose of teaching us about our greatest strength: LOVE. It may sound hippie-hippie or woo-woo, but it is really the most basic truth. Deep in my heart, I know that there is so much more love, joy, and abundance that can be experienced by all. But like every story, there are extreme challenges that must be overcome in order for the heroes to emerge and create ultimate victory and glory for all.

Among my favorite Sanskrit mantras, this one has been passed down through the lineages of yoga: *"Lokah Samastah*

Sukhino Bhavantu." It means: "May all beings be happy and free. And may my thoughts, words and actions help to create that happiness and freedom for all." We must remember that each of us is here for a purpose, so we should strive to live in that truth every day. It's this truth that will bring happiness to us all, within and without.

I share this story so that you may be inspired, you may understand that there is always challenge and struggle in the human form, and that the only constant in our lives is change. When we can approach this change with love and gratitude, that we can continue to receive all of the blessings that life has to offer us. I am so grateful for all that I am and the woman I have become, and for those who have not only supported me on my path, but also challenged me. All are my teachers.

Growing up in Charlotte, North Carolina, I was extremely shy as a child. I always felt like I didn't belong, because I looked different than most of the other kids in school. My mother is of Chinese-Hawaiian ancestry, and was born and raised in Hawaii with island roots, and my father is a caucasian southern gentleman of English/Scottish descent.

While my parents gave their three children plenty of love, I received a confusing mix of exotic island wildness with conservative southern hospitality and elegance. We did all of the things that a "good" Southern family "should" do; go to school, get good grades, go to church, play after school sports and be involved in community activities. My favorite class was always art, where I could create things with my hands. I loved that with each art project, there was a multitude of possibilities, an infinite number of creations, and that everyone's work turned out as a unique expression of herself. I like that I had the ability to find my own source of creativity from within. When I wasn't creating art, my younger sister Emilia and I would play dress up, sing and dance together, and we would play games outside with our older brother Christopher and the other kids in the neighborhood. I played competitive sports: soccer, swimming, cross country and softball, which gave me a sense of discipline, being a team player, and athleticism.

Every summer, my mother would take the kids (my older brother, myself and my younger sister) back to her childhood home in Honolulu. There, we would visit our grandparents for about one month. We spent our days playing in the waves of Waikiki and exploring the islands with our extended *Ohana* (family). Coming to Hawaii every year was like coming home; I belonged, not only because I looked like my cousins, but because I didn't feel judged for my differences - like the outsider that I felt I was back home in Charlotte. At the end of summer when it was time to leave our island home, we would all cry at the airport, feeling as though we were leaving a piece of our hearts in Hawaii.

One Christmas, my aunt Helene gifted me a beading kit. It had small seed beads, fishing line and clasps. I would spend hours alone in my bedroom making beaded bracelets and necklaces for my friends and myself. I enjoyed the meditative silence which allowed me to still my mind and completely focus on the process of creativity. I loved becoming a designer and watching my pieces come to life on different bodies.

Separation

Like many Americans, I was encouraged to attend college because it was the acceptable thing to do. I was accepted into a very prestigious school in Virginia. Even though I didn't know what I wanted to study, I was excited to be on my own. I lost myself in the social scene, trying to discover who I was. For the first year and a half of college, I partied hard, drank a lot of alcohol, and experimented with a variety of drugs. It was also in college that I attended my first yoga classes with friends. But I felt too uncomfortable focusing on my breath and my posture, and listening to my thoughts; so I quit after attending a few classes, swearing I would never go back.

I started to become depressed. I didn't feel like I had any real purpose, or direction. I had constantly been told what to do my entire life, and now that I had to make decisions, it was scary becoming an adult and facing reality. Alongside my friends, I started to use drugs and alcohol as a way to find happiness. I felt a lack of sincere connection and eventually I knew I needed something different. I longed for a change: warmth, expression, culture, inspiration.

I signed up for a study abroad program in Costa Rica to further my Spanish skills and take a break from the harsh winter in the Blue Ridge Mountains of Virginia. I was nervous about taking off on a solo adventure as a 19 year-old woman; but I sensed there was more to see and learn beyond what I could imagine. I moved in with a host family and began my studies. I traveled around the country to discover the many beaches that my heart longed to explore. Because I didn't know anyone, there were no expectations of me. I was free to do whatever I wanted. I challenged myself; to learn, to grow and to step out of my comfort zone - because I had to learn how to communicate in Spanish in order to get by. It was during this time that I rekindled my love for design and I first learned how to surf. I began dating a *Tico* (Costa Rican man), a traveling artisan who sold his handcrafted jewelry and accessories around the country. I appreciated the simplicity of his life, though it was very different from mine. He was happy being creative and traveling for a living. He offered me my first lessons in wire-wrapping with pliers. I would travel by bus to meet him on the weekends in different parts of the country. *Pura vida*.

When I returned to school in Virginia, I was a changed woman. I had seen a different world than what the affluent, white-collar community in this small private school experienced. School felt restrictive and stagnant. I had a hard time connecting with my friends, who were still heavily involved in the party scene. My soul had expanded in such a way that I no longer fit into the same box I'd inhabited before. I had learned to enjoy the freedom and beauty of a larger perspective in a new land, where culture and expression thrive. I soon quit sorority life to spend my free time doing what I loved: designing jewelry. Once again, just as in my childhood, I saw my ability to create as a quality that I enjoyed expressing.

The following year in school, I longed to return to in Central America. So I signed up to do service work in Nicaragua, during spring break..I was going to build compostable latrines, homes and sustainable gardens for impoverished communities. Meanwhile, my friends and classmates had begun to notice my unique designs, so I began selling my jewelry at school events in order to raise funds for the trip. The proceeds of my sales successfully funded my subsequent trips to Nicaragua, where I was able to make a huge difference to impoverished communities. For them, to have American students come to help them gave them hope and inspiration, feelings of support from people they didn't even know. My heart felt full by being able to share my gifts; by seeing how my creativity was appreciated by my fellow students and across the world. And being able to fund my humanitarian trip to Nicaragua was an added benefit of abundance. My work was serving people in a grander way than I realized.

My college experience could have wound up completely different, based on my choices. During my senior year, I contacted a friend to buy some weed from him. He came over and sold me some marijuana. Before he left, he stuffed something I didn't recognize into a little glass pipe, placed the pipe a few inches away from my face, and politely asked,

"Would you like to try some?"

"What is it?" I asked.

"Crystal meth. ICE. It gets you so high," he answered.

I saw my life flash in front of my eyes as I remembered my uncle and all he had been through. I remember the day my mom told us (children) that her younger brother had been addicted to crystal meth for many years. I appreciated my mom's unfiltered truth that she shared. I had witnessed, first-hand, how his addiction and aggressive behavior affected our entire family.

"No thanks," I responded to my friend.

In 2005, upon graduating *magna cum laude* with a double major in Spanish and studio art, I planned to start a company. I wasn't addicted to drugs or alcohol, like many of my classmates, nor, thankfully, had I ever been sexually assaulted, like so many college students. I considered myself a success story. My father strongly encouraged me to get a real job with benefits and a salary since I hadn't taken any classes in marketing, business, economics or accounting. But I wanted to be an entrepreneur. I briefly moved back in with my parents in Charlotte to save money and start my business. I built a simple website and hosted pop-up events at my mother's friends' homes. So began my career in jewelry design.

On my 22nd birthday, a few months after college graduation, my long-time college boyfriend broke up with me. I was heartbroken and depressed. I had dedicated so much time to our relationship, and we had planned out our entire future together. I thought he was *the one*, and that we would end up happily ever after. I couldn't eat, I had no motivation, and I would sleep the days away. What was the point of life? The one thing that kept me going was my dream to move to Hawaii to be with my brother and sister who were both living there. The desire to save up enough money to make it to Hawaii kept me designing jewelry and booking shows.

Over the next six months, I saved up enough money to buy a plane ticket to Hawaii, where I would live my dream of being a surfer girl. No more cold, harsh winters on the East Coast. I moved to Hawaii on Christmas Eve 2005; a gift to myself! I moved into my mother's childhood home in Honolulu, with my brother, sister, and 76 year-old Hawaiian-Chinese grandmother. I began selling my jewelry at local craft fairs and farmers' markets, while modeling bikinis part time, and promoting liquor for distributors. I supplemented the income from my jewelry design career with the extra work, spending my money on rent, food, and more beads!

I soon met the future father of my child. Chris was handsome and fun; and we were wildly in lustful love. We moved to the 'country' of the North Shore, known for its big, beautiful waves and a lifestyle far different from the city. I quickly became pregnant, and out of obligation, we married. When I was about three months pregnant, our next door neighbor, Red Mahan, (now a dear friend of mine) introduced me to the idea of home birth. It sounded absolutely crazy! At his suggestion and after researching the possibility, I watched Ricki Lake's documentary: "The Business of Being Born." Watching that film made me feel empowered. I knew that, just as my ancestors had done in centuries past, I too had the power to birth my baby in a natural way. As women, our bodies are designed to reproduce. I trusted in the power of my body and my ability to grow this baby inside of me. So I felt strongly that I could also give birth to my baby in the comfort of my home.

As an overwhelmingly maternal instinct began to kick in, I shifted my lifestyle. I started to eat healthier foods and began taking prenatal yoga classes in order to meet other pregnant women. I found a midwife that I loved, and soon discovered that I had serious medical issues with my cervix that required attention. But treatment would have to wait until after childbirth.

Chris and I spent the summer together playing in the ocean, swimming with dolphins, and focusing on our respective careers. The day I went into labor, I was 36.5 weeks pregnant. I walked my dog at the beach and lounged around the house. Chris helped me to shift into comfortable positions during contractions. Using my breath, I moaned loudly throughout the contractions, which helped me surrender to the birthing process, getting out of my own mind, and into my body.

Our midwife was summoned after 17 hours of labor. When she arrived, I was on all fours on the living room floor, circling my hips and moaning. I wouldn't consider the feelings I experienced as pain, but rather intense sensations. The midwife suggested that I sit on the toilet to "move things along." Labor began to progress rapidly because my body intuitively knew to relax on the toilet. At one point, I thought it was physically impossible to get the baby out naturally. I remember having an out-of-body experience where I could see the entire scene from an outside perspective. I began to unintentionally push while on the toilet. Chris swiftly picked me up and placed me onto a birthing stool a few feet away. Dr. Lori dove under me to catch the baby. Then, with one loud, orgasmic sound, I pushed my baby out and into the arms of my midwife below me. She passed him to me, with the cord still intact and connected to the placenta inside my womb. My labor lasted 19 hours, but I was so energized. As soon as my newborn son was in my arms, I felt the most intense love and happiness that I have ever felt in my life. The natural hormone oxytocin, the love hormone, the hormone of orgasm and bliss, was flowing through my body; I felt like I could have repeated that experience over and over again. I was so in love.

Although I experienced an amazing and empowering birth with my son Aukai, the feelings of loneliness and isolation after birth caused me to experience postpartum depression. I have never felt so alone as I did during my baby's first few months of life. His father was doing what most dads do; leaving for work early in the morning and coming home in the evening. I was left alone with this new baby, in a new home, in a new community, barely able to fend for myself. Trying to accomplish the simplest tasks, such as brushing my teeth or going for a pee, were challenging with a baby in tow - let alone cooking up a healthy meal so I could provide my baby with nutritious breast milk. My hormones were out of balance because I didn't eat my placenta – from which I would have obtained important nutrients that are needed after birth. All mammals eat their placentas after delivery. (I would definitely eat my placenta next time around if I ever have another baby.)

I felt unsupported emotionally, physically and spiritually; and my son's father and I were arguing a lot. Our relationship was very tumultuous and caused me a lot of pain, as we were both having a very difficult time adjusting to being new parents. I judged myself for not living up to society's standards and expectations of a happy family. I also placed a lot of blame on Chris, because I didn't want to admit to the truth of getting married out of obligation rather than love. I started to play the victim, and became defensive and angry with him.

We decided to get divorced since we didn't really want to be together. Going to family court to decide custody over our son was one of the most challenging times of my life. I felt attacked as a mother because of his false claims that I was negligent and abusive. I had done my best and given my son everything I had, for months on end; but I still felt abandoned while Chris was at work all day.

I was traumatized to the point where I questioned my abilities, my intentions, and my worth. I knew in my heart that I was a good mother, but whenever I was verbally attacked, the self-doubt crept back in. After considerable expense and months of lawyer's visits, I was awarded full custody. Thankfully a visitation schedule was set into place by the judge, establishing boundaries; it also provided me with a *mama* vacation every summer, and for a few weeks every year. I was able to set a travel schedule for myself and my new partner at the time. Even though the divorce triggered a lot of fearful emotions, it was actually a blessing after all. The things that challenge us most can make us stronger, and can become our greatest teachers. The passage from maiden to motherhood had shifted something inside of me. This was the start of my journey towards feeling like a sovereign, empowered, beautiful woman.

Once Chris and I divorced, it felt as if the dark and stormy clouds of negativity had passed. A friend introduced me to Louise Hay's Power Thought Cards deck, and I began repeating affirmations such as: "I am prosperous and the Universe is abundant." I was struggling financially on my own, and after paying rent, I only had a few hundred dollars left with were barely enough for me to provide for my son. Initially, I didn't believe in the power of affirmations. But I continued to practice the power of words, because I felt that it was the only way to help me move forward. Life had blessed me with a beautiful, healthy baby and a life in Hawaii. Aukai was so sweet and we loved each other. He was developing his sense of humor, and he enjoyed having fun with me. I had hoped to breastfeed for at least a year, and I had reached my goal. When he was 14 months old, I decided to wean him off breastfeeding, so that I could have a little more independence. I put my son in daycare, part-time, so I could focus on my work more. I also traded babysitter services for jewelry. With such rapid changes happening, I was determined to focus on the good and what I wanted to create in my life.

I began to attend beach workout classes alongside other moms and babies, as well as more yoga classes with friends. We all supported each other and understood the challenges that arise from a lack of sleep and exhaustion, as well as our new roles: butt wipers and milk maids. I also began to take ukulele lessons so I could practice using my voice (just as I had loved to sing with my sister in childhood) and learn the new skill of playing an instrument. I loved the feeling of creating melodies with my fingertips and using my voice to sing to my baby. My mother had played Hawaiian music during my childhood in North Carolina, to remind her of her beautiful island home. I soon began to learn those songs so as to connect with my own Hawaiian heritage. I felt empowered to develop another mode of expression, and a way to soothe my son to sleep. Plus, I had always secretly dreamed of being a musician one day, and this could be a great start!

Life had begun anew. My health, my strong supportive friendships, my yoga practice, surfing, and the power of affirmations became key to my happiness and survival.

I knew it was time to take care of my cervix, which I had put on the back-burner since pregnancy. I sought medical advice, and my doctor recommended an invasive procedure in which a chunk of my cervix would be cut out. She tried to persuade me to do the suggested treatment, saying that, without it, I would develop cervical cancer within the next few years. I felt upset that the standard procedure was to simply cut out the problem rather than to discover the root of the issue. I decided to get a second opinion, and I sought alternative treatment for my cervix from a local naturopath. Using a variety of natural supplements and non-surgical treatments, I was healed within four weeks! It was almost unbelievable that my body had responded so well. But I also felt empowered in following my intuition to heal my body from within. I am so grateful I made that decision, because upon further research, I discovered that many women experience infertility and other issues related to this standard medical treatment of cutting the cervix. Unlike my original doctor had suggested, I haven't gotten cervical cancer and my pap smears have all been normal since!

Life just kept getting better once I had followed my intuition and was living in my truth. Within a few days of Chris moving out, a team from a Japanese TV show, *Aloha Tengoku*, came to my home to interview me and feature my work on their program. This exposure put me on the map as an internationally recognized Hawaiian designer, and marked the beginning of a long and prosperous relationship with Japanese customers.

My affirmation practice of calling in abundance began to manifest as many fruitful business opportunities appeared. After being featured in a multitude of magazines, guidebooks, television and radio shows, I found more retail boutiques that wanted to carry my jewelry line. I was also invited to Japan to participate in the "Love Hawaii" festival in Yokohama. Since I didn't speak the language, I was very nervous to visit Japan for the first time. After years of following a simple island lifestyle, finding myself in a big city was extremely intimidating. Not to mention that I was leaving my three year old son behind with family, and would be traveling solo! At the festival, I was showered with so much love from all of my Japanese fans. I delighted in the popularity of my work; I had no idea that I could affect people across the world in such a way. The aloha spirit that I intentionally embedded into my creations was being received by my customers, and was feeding their souls while also feeding my own desire to express my own creativity. Through interactions with Japanese customers over the years, I have gained a deeper understanding of their beautiful culture. I am honored to know that my work can, despite a language barrier, create so much joy, beauty and connection.

As my business continued to blossom, I needed assistance! At the suggestion of my good friend, I hired my first employees to help grow my business. I soon moved my home office into a garage that belonged to my friend and childhood surf idol Rochelle Ballard. I began dating a sweet and handsome man named Dusty, who became a wonderful father figure to my son, who helped to build out the new space. Rochelle had a yoga studio on her property, and I started practicing more yoga to balance out my busy work schedule and as a way to find peace of mind. One day, at a kundalini yoga class, Romey, the teacher, invited us to sing a sacred mantra. I had never chanted a mantra before, and as I began to sing with the group, tears poured down my cheeks. I felt a huge sense of relief with the release of so much pain, fear and sadness that had been stored in my body from the last few years of pregnancy, marriage, childbirth and divorce. I had been moving so quickly through life that I hadn't fully processed all of my feelings. Chanting that one mantra opened up a portal in my life. It sent me on a spiraling journey of empowerment and self-growth. It also set me on my true path as a yogini and teacher. I still didn't really understand the meaning of "yoga,", but I felt strongly that I needed to dive deeper into the practice.

With no intention of becoming a teacher, I enrolled in a 200-hour Kundalini yoga teacher training course in India. During the training in India, my emotions were flowing as my world back home in Hawaii was literally being turned upside down. My son's father continually accused me of being a neglectful mother, (meanwhile he wasn't paying any child support,) and Rochelle had sold her property, which meant that I had to move out of her garage as soon as I returned to Hawaii. The yogic practices of *pranayama* (breath work), *asana* (physical postures), *mantras* (chants), and the support from my ashram roommate Erica Jago kept me feeling present, safe and alive. It was there that I began to combine ukulele melodies with these ancient mantras (that have literally been chanted for thousands of years as a form of devotion and prayer) as a way to explore my voice and practice what I was learning. I kept the energy moving out through my voice, just as I had been taught by my teacher Gurmukh: "Noelani, just keep playing your ukulele." I vividly remember walking back to the ashram after class one day. I played my ukulele as I sang: "The universe is manifesting something greater than I can even imagine." I was scared of what the future held, but I trusted that everything was going to be just fine.

Upon my return to Hawaii, things moved quickly. I decided to pursue my lifelong dream of opening up a retail boutique since I needed to move locations anyway. I had always been afraid to step into the position of store owner, but the Universe pushed me into the role without any alternatives. After many late night discussions with my partner, I signed a lease on the old Pizza Hut building in our town within a month of my return from India. With Dusty's support and carpentry skills, combined with my desire to teach, we decided to build out the space as a yoga studio and retail boutique. I had a deep desire to teach yoga, and share my jewelry on a whole new level, while empowering my community.

I loved creating this new space in our sleepy little town. I began teaching a few classes/week, and sharing my ukulele mantra music with my students. This was a big shift from my timid childhood personality. Even though the yoga philosophies and practices I shared were so new to me in this lifetime, teaching felt natural. It was as if I had lived these truths for centuries, and they were finally being called back into my spirit. My son even loved practicing acro-yoga with me, and enjoyed when I sang the mantras to lull him to sleep. I loved bringing my students into sacred song, and they constantly shared with me how open-hearted they felt after singing – much as I had felt in my first Kundalini class.

The yoga studio and boutique became a catalyst for change in our community; allowing people to feel empowered, expressive and connected in our space. Women were coming in to receive activations of beauty and love with my crystal jewelry line and wearable art pieces. Our studio and boutique became a haven with a multitude of offerings, where women would simply come by to find peace of mind. We had multiple teachers offering many styles of yoga, and I began leading sound healing with crystal bowls, toning practices, and mantras. I was asked to be a featured presenter at Wanderlust Festival Oahu in 2015, and sang alongside one of my idols, Nahko Bear. I dreamed of one day recording an album with all of the music that was starting to express itself through me. But running the boutique, teaching yoga, designing jewelry - all while being a mother - was more than a full time job. I also still had much to learn about the music industry, which seemed daunting and impossible.

While I was learning a lot about business, social media and customer service in a whole new dimension, I was also feeling overwhelmed and exhausted from managing my business in it's new commercial setting. I decided to embark on a five week international adventure with the goal of expanding my perspective and education by accomplishing two tasks; completing a 200-hour sound-based mantra yoga teacher training in India with Anandra George; and assisting my friend Meredith Rom at her women's yoga retreat in Bali. Diving into the heart of sound with 15 other students expanded my heart's capacity to love even more. We studied mantra and sound which brought me so much clarity and presence. I would sit by the River Ganga and play my ukulele and write songs. I set the intention on that full moon in April of 2016 to record a mantra album, finally. I left for Bali to assist at the women's retreat but had a few days to explore on my own before the retreat began.

A friend from Hawaii had suggested that I go to Ecstatic Dance at Yoga Barn in the town of Ubud. I had no idea what ecstatic dance was, but it sounded fun, so upon his suggestion of arriving early, I showed up 45 minutes prior to class, and tickets were sold out! I was so frustrated after having spent two and a half hours in traffic to get there. I surrendered to beauty, to gratitude, to blessings. Chanting the mantras that I learned in India kept me present: there's got to be a way to get into the dance. *Om gam ganapataye namaha.* Then I saw him...the DJ, the guy who could get me in. Unashamed because I had nothing to lose, I approached him at the front desk, and asked him if he would put me on *the list.* "Sure." he responded. Sweet! Within all of the blocks, an opening. I danced my booty off and was so high on life. DJ Raio happened to be a producer, and he helped me to record my first two songs in his studio in Bali. If I hadn't taken that chance...and asked for help getting into the dance, what would have happened? The Universe supports us, but we must choose to take the steps needed. I returned to my home in Hawaii with the beginnings of my first album. After supporting the women during their personal transformations at the retreat, I began leading bi-monthly (full and new) moon women's circles on the North Shore where I lived, and I was also inspired to host my first international women's retreat.

Every time I travel, I experience growth and evolution; knowledge is gained, attachments are lost, and I return home feeling grateful, refreshed, and inspired. I return ready to integrate my knowledge into my life here, and to share these gifts with my friends and community. Coming back to Hawaii is a gift, as it is truly a paradise. We have the beautiful ocean, the swaying palm trees, the most amazing sunsets, and a beach that is our playground. But what I have come to realize through my trainings, through my own practice and in my own life, is that paradise can be found anywhere. I didn't need to have my own boutique space to be happy anymore.

For nearly five years, the boutique proved to be a fun way to share my offerings, and allowed me to make a decent living. But over time, I had outgrown it. Traffic on my commute to work was increasing; I wasn't spending enough time with my quickly growing son; and I wanted to focus on my music. I was constantly asking myself: What do I need in order to feed my own soul? What keeps me inspired? Quality time with my son, reading, writing, yoga, design, surfing, travel and music!

I was again feeling restricted and ready for growth and evolution. It felt like the boutique, as well as my seven year relationship with my partner had come to a point of completion. I easily could have stayed in the relationship and kept working at the boutique and studio. But in my heart, I knew that was not what I wanted to be doing anymore. I needed to expand beyond my comfort levels and explore my potential.

Continually listening to my soul's calling and rebuilding after the breakdowns is where the magic happens.

As of this writing, it has been six months since I closed my shop, ended my relationship and I am about to launch my first album, Lakshmi Lullabies. The album is a compilation of Hawaiian, Sanskrit, and Kundalini yoga mantras which I hope will inspire many to sing along and explore their voices. I am grateful for the lessons learned in my relationship and in owning my boutique, as well as the courage to lovingly release those things that no longer serve my highest. Where will I go now? What do I see happening?

I am about to return to Bali (with my 10 year old son) to perform at Bali Spirit Festival, joined by my sister Emilia and my dear friends who will create our band on stage! Next month, I will launch a new Goddess Collection of jewelry designs in alignment with the release of my album. I will lead two international women's retreats this year. I see myself traveling more and sharing my jewelry, yoga and music with people around the world. I see myself surrounded by inspiring individuals so that I can continue inspiring and supporting people to realize that they are sovereign, creative beings with gifts to share and more creative power than they can imagine. I wish to activate these powers within my fellow brothers and sisters to create more harmony and peace on the earth. Let's visualize this together.

My name is Noelani Love. I am a woman, a mother, a daughter, a granddaughter, a sister.

I am a servant on this Earth home.

Like you, I am a human doing my best to survive with the knowledge I have gained through life's challenges, from my parents, teachers, society and cultural conditioning. What I am learning now is how to be most in touch with my spirit and how to listen to the guide inside. Here I am. Whole. Full, Unbroken. Raw. Vulnerable. Sovereign. Me. A blessing. A miracle. Kinetic energy in the form of a human with a soul inside. I am my muse.

"How does one become a butterfly?" she asked. You must want to fly so much that you are willing to give up being a caterpillar."

~ Trina Paulus

CHAPTER 6

Caterpillar To Butterfly. I once could crawl but now I can FLY!

By Jeanetta Matichak

Let's think about and picture the image of a beautiful caterpillar that is fuzzy and cute crawling around on the ground. He is very limited to what he might be able to see and do. His vision is limited to his environment and he can't get too far into other spaces of the world to see what might be available to this being. Now let's think about the butterfly. That same being is now transformed into something that is brilliantly beautiful who can fly anywhere and see the world from all aspects and edges of space. Can you see the vast difference of just his vision? Once he could only see a limited amount of the world, and now he can fly he can see anything he chooses.

As you take this journey with me, I want you to see yourself today as the caterpillar, and by the end of this time together I want you to be the free butterfly. Maybe you are already the butterfly and don't even realize it. Wherever you are in your life, take this ride of a lifetime with me and just be open to exploring freedom, love, harmony, laughter, and peace and moving away from fear, anger, and frustration.

I invite you to look through a new lens into your life as you listen to this adventure and see how the detours and obstacles are the marvelous teachers. These adventures assisted the caterpillar to become the butterfly. Many times in our lives, we look at the difficult times as the biggest challenges and setbacks, when actually they are the best teachers and can propel us into becoming the new beings we are meant to be. When you can look at hardships as marvelous teachers, then you have journeyed into loving your life and setting yourself free, like a butterfly, to explore and love any space you are in. That is my wish for you as we take this time together: that you can look at your life differently once we have walked this path together, and that you can look through a different lens. You can love the difficult times and know you are meant to be right where you are in this moment in time. Loving your life and living in peace is the healthiest place to be.

Let's take a journey back in time. There was this little girl (me) who lived as if she were living alone. She had a home and food provided by a caring family. She was well cared for and properly given all that is needed to survive. There was still something missing. Being given food and shelter to survive is one thing, but being given emotional love and support is another thing to thrive. When I was only five, my parents decided to divorce, which at that time was probably healthier for the entire household, rather than the fighting, yelling, door slamming, and drinking that was being done by my father.

This man, a Vietnam veteran, was 90% disabled from what his physical body and mental body encountered while giving his life to the military. He was losing his battle with life due to the demons that were constantly engulfing him from his time spent in Vietnam. To deal with his difficulties, he daily turned to alcohol to assist him in coping not only with his physical pain, which was intense because part of his body being blown up, but also his mental pain from what he experienced while he was there.

Prior to his leaving for the war, he and my mother were blissfully in love. Absolutely crazy in love and ready to take on the world together. They were soulmates and knew they had found something special in each other. When I think about this situation, it allows me to have gratitude for everyone and everything in my life. They had no idea what the future had in store for them. If they had only known, they probably would have run in the other direction. Use this piece of history to remind yourself how precious life is and that each day is a gift. Treat it as a present and cherish it with all of your being. I have learned to live loving my life in the moment and being grateful for right now. It has truly helped this caterpillar become a butterfly. It is far too easy to worry about the future and stress about the past. ***Choose.*** That is the important word here. CHOOSE to be present in this day and love it as if it were your last.

Moving on with the story, my parents got divorced. My father moved out and his alcoholism took over. He was hanging onto life by a thread of his being. We would barely see him, and when we did, it was pure bliss for me. I knew the feeling of being safe in my father's arms; it was a feeling I longed for daily. When he did show up and I would get just minutes in his arms, it was a feeling that was unexplainable. As a child, I had no idea what this feeling was, just that in those moments I was with him and snuggling, it was as if time stopped and love was pouring into my soul. Then, he would leave and it would be a long time before I would see him, and I would feel lost and empty. During this time in my life, my mother was doing the best she could. I was feeling isolated and disconnected from my mother and brother. I was wanting emotional connection but didn't know how to get it. Thus, sometimes I would act out just to get attention from my mother. I was surviving in my life but not thriving. My brother would joke with me about how I was adopted, and I think my child-mind might have actually believed that. I felt as if I was not wanted. This was never my mother's intention, but these were my own thoughts swirling, the thoughts of a lonely child.

My father died due to his body just giving up from all of the obstacles he was dealing with. A memory of standing at this coffin, touching his body, putting my hand on his face for the last time, is something I can see clearly in my mind still to this day. I remember standing there thinking," I will never know this man that I loved so much. I will never feel that amazing feeling of pure bliss that I had only in his arms, and I will never be in his presence again." This rocked my world as a little girl. I had no one I could explain my feelings to and truly might not have been able to really express them as I was feeling. I would scream out loud at God and ask him why? Why my father? Why did this happen to my family? Why now? My mother was so checked out of my emotional needs and I needed this man to be here for me in some capacity. I remember throwing stuffed animals at my wall and crying in torture of how badly it hurt to know I would never have that feeling again.

I felt alone, abandoned, isolated, and lost. My brother and I had a typical sibling relationship. Therefore, I felt as if I had just been left to experience this world on my own. My young mind was torturing me daily with sadness, anger, bitterness, depression; my emotions were running a roller coaster on me. For you do not know and understand what you don't know! Transformation starts in the mind. If you are living from this place of loneliness, lack, anger, and fear, then that is what you will see and feel all day long every day.

STOP and think about this right now. If you are living in fear and unhappiness, that is what you are going to get every day. You are inviting this focus on the energy of having nothing and being nothing. Then you are nothing. What you think about all day long is what you are inviting into your mind. Thoughts become your reality. I was feeling and thinking that I was worthless, life was hopeless, and no one loved me. I believed my father was the one person who loved me, and he was gone. I felt abandoned and lost. I felt like no one understood me or even cared to understand my feelings. Those are heavy feelings to be dealing with as a child.

My childhood of feeling abandoned turned into many years of running after things, people, and places to fill this intensely large hole I had in my heart. I was alone on so many levels. I was lonely with my own mind constantly talking negatively to me. I was feeling like no one cared, understood me, or even tried. My mother and brother were constantly calling me selfish and mean. I was living from a place in my head that felt hopeless. I decided I was the only person I could count on. I could not count on my family, my friends, or anyone in my life. Thus, I was living from a low state of anger, bitterness, and hate.

This would soon take a very hard toll on me. I was drinking heavily as a teenager, eventually taking drugs of all kinds and looking for love from anyone who would give me attention. One can only imagine the disaster this brings. In your biggest imagination, yes, all of those things were happening and then some. I try not to even go back to the thoughts and actions involved in those days, because it feels like a dream. It was not who I am and was never who I wanted to be. My self-worth was not intact. Who was I? Why did I not love myself enough to say no? I don't think I believed I could. I didn't believe in myself, nor that I was strong enough, good enough, or powerful enough to even stand up for myself. I also wanted to be loved so badly that I would take it in any form, even if it that meant to be treated badly. I allowed people to treat me unkindly because I had no idea how to say no, and I also just wanted to feel loved.

Have you ever felt like this? Have you doubted yourself? Who you are? Have you felt like no one in your life really cared about you? This was the negative record that was playing over and over in my head on a daily basis for years. It played on repeat until the magic happened.

What, you ask, was the magic? What was the turning of tides in my life that completely changed it all? It was the best teacher and gift of my life. You see sometimes we have to go through complete hell to find out who we are meant to be in this life. I truly believe that. I went through something so challenging that it ALMOST took my life, and it should have! I was broken and felt so defeated that I wanted it all to end. I was done trying to put on this happy face that was a complete mask of the pain I was dealing with inside. For so long, I had hidden and suppressed these emotions of my childhood in order to protect myself, but really this inability to face my pain was killing me. This was the programming that I had used my entire life to deal with my pain. The programming in my head was how I would protect myself.

Then I stepped into a situation in which life took the biggest turn of living hell on earth. Looking back now, I realize that what you are thinking all day long is what you create. I was thinking I was not good enough, and then I invited the biggest storm into my life. This storm, as I will only ever explain, is the one that should have swept me up and taken me away. That is how intense it was, how much bigger than me it was. This storm was devastating and disastrous. It was sent to be the storm that forever transformed my life. At the time, I thought it was the storm that was sent to end my life, end my marriage, and destroy all that I had and was.

Do you ever look back at your life and realize the obstacles that were meant to break you were actually the ones that made you who you are today? They made you stronger than you could have ever dreamed possible. If you don't believe that to be true, please learn from my story. I should not be here sharing this with you. I tried to commit suicide due to the darkness I was dealing with. I should not be alive on this earth breathing and telling of my transformation. Not only did this storm destroy me so much that I wanted to end my life, but for a while after, I had those thoughts over and over again. My mind was in a constant state of fear. I felt like my brain was a beehive on fire. This beehive was buzzing all day long, and then when the storm hit it was on fire. That is the best description I can give which explains the torment that I was feeling daily in my mind.

It was only from the renewing of my mind and the transformation of my thoughts that I became clear and EVERYTHING changed. You may be asking, How did this happen? How did this horrible storm come in and destroy you and then all of a sudden everything changed you? I definitely believe in miracles, and I see them happen daily now. I allowed this storm to come in. I was living from a place of unhappiness and bitterness. When we are living in a state of lonely thoughts and lack of worth, we do not realize we are allowing any and all thoughts to take us captive. We are welcoming in those negative emotions, and then, when they appear, we wonder how they got there. They got there because thoughts create experiences. The fear we let in becomes reality. We choose what to think about all day long and that is what we become. These thoughts may not show up in your life exactly as you are thinking them. It is possible for it to show up even darker than you perceive in your mind. Your mind is very powerful. Maybe I should say that again: your mind is very powerful! Did you hear me? Your mind is VERY powerful.

For me, the day everything changed will forever be remembered as the day God transformed my mind and I was set free from the bondage. I had tried to end my life and I awoke the next morning not even sure of where I was. I didn't know if I was dead or dreaming. When I first awoke, I didn't know if I had left this world, because my mind was so foggy. Shortly after waking up, I realized I was still here on earth and I was alive. I was almost disappointed for a few seconds.

I also want to help others understand that, in this place of torment, in my mind, I was never able to think about my family and the difficult circumstances this would bring on them. I was unable to think about the impact my death would have on them. Granted, I have lost my entire family to cancer and I know the depths of grief all too well. In this mental state I was in, I could never have worried about them. I know that might sound very selfish, but during the darkest hours of your mental torment, you are not able to worry about how this might affect your loved ones. I think about this all too often when I hear of individuals committing suicide. People chose to gossip and ridicule the selfishness that suicide has on them, but do they ever think about what the individual was dealing with? I am here to remind you, that is not something I could even focus on when I was feeling the darkness of mind. I think, due to the torment I was feeling daily in my thoughts, I could not even think about what my actions would do to others. I could only deal with the ever so challenging things I was thinking and feeling. This is something I want to share that is very real and raw. It may paint me to look as if I have no heart for my actions or for what I could have done, but in those moments, and many other times, I could not see past the fog and the darkness. In those times, I could not think about my family and how it would affect them. I could only think about the horrible thoughts that were circling in my mind. The constant replay and the heaviness that came with this storm was paralyzing to my body. I felt as if I was dragging around 500 pounds of bricks. The deep ache and pain that sets in when I would awake each morning, the feeling of terror and torment of just wanting to escape this life, the darkness that lives on in your thoughts each moment, of just wanting to have peace, the bitterness of watching others feel joy and longing for that feeling...does this paint the picture for you? Can you understand or relate to these feelings?

Thus, after I awoke and finally came to realize I was alive and I had been given the opportunity to live, I found myself sitting in the bathtub, still where I had passed out the night before, and I knew without any doubt that God had saved me for a reason. I knew my life had a purpose and I was meant to be here for something. I quickly prayed in that bathtub for God to use me to help others. I prayed for peace, forgiveness, and clarity for my path.

This day was the beginning of my transformation into a new life here on earth. I wasn't quite sure what that new life would look like or even be, but I knew I was going to be used to help others. In the days to come and months that passed, there were ups and downs that would come and go. I was dealing with life from a new lens and could be a bit more patient with myself and my emotions. I was trying to figure out why my mind played tricks on me at times and why my emotions were so paralyzing from time to time. I have gone through intense counseling to deal with the storm. I was going through all of the documents that I had collected from the doctors, therapists, and psychiatrist. I was trying to piece together the puzzle that was now my life.

In the next months to come, I was trying to get my life back together and to move forward by picking up the pieces of this puzzle called life. I was living for the first time and looking at myself through a new lens called love. I was thinking about all the negative things I have dealt with in my life and looking at myself with love for the first time ever. Why is this so crazy to think about? I think because I'd never loved who I was for so many reasons. I dealt with fear, shame, anger, and bitterness towards myself since I was a child, never understanding why I would make the decisions I made and then living with regret or shame in what happened as a result. I was hating who I was for most of my life but not knowing why I would walk the most difficult path in front of me. Why would I choose to go down the path that would bring such destruction in my life?

Learning to love myself meant learning how to release such judgement about who I thought I was and who I truly was deep in my soul. I had never before been taught what self-love meant. I had always looked at loving myself as being selfish. I was not taught that my own feelings mattered and that what I thought in my mind was important. I'd had this negative programming going on in my mind since I was a child, telling me that I was not good enough or worthy enough to be heard. Thus, that came about in my actions, as it was okay to let others hurt me and I couldn't stand up for what was right. This was a bad cycle I had gotten into.

Have you ever dealt with something like this? Do you question where it came from? I believe that I picked up these thoughts in my childhood from how I was treated and then I replayed them in my mind over and over. I do not believe these were my thoughts, but I created them because of the way I had been treated. It could also be from being told I was a selfish being from the time I was little. This played over and over in my head. Also, there was the fear of believing I was adopted and not wanted. Think about the program you have created in your mind that has been playing since you were a child. What does it look like? What does it sound like?

Therefore, as time went on, I was learning more about emotions and feelings which I had never studied before. I started to read books upon books about everything and anything dealing with any topic that connected to self-love, psychology, emotions, and feelings. I became almost obsessed in getting to the bottom of what I was going through. I was circling my life in my head every day trying to recall past events and then putting together pieces of the puzzle. I wrote a book titled *Finding Peace* to help me and others understand that life is all about being in the present and living with gratitude. Even through the writing of this book, I was still looking for what I was not finding which was complete peace, love, harmony, and joy. I was getting moments of peace, but then it was followed by moments or days of darkness. I would meditate, exercise, go for long walks, and try anything to get back into that tranquil place and still long for that feeling of complete peace.

I felt almost like a hypocrite at times, because here I had written this amazing book on peace and I was still not finding it regularly. It was during these days that I would not give up on seeking how to find the joy that I was missing. Why had I been feeling much better and then, all of a sudden, I was back in this dark hole that felt bigger and darker than it ever had? I was supposed to be at peace, and that just wasn't happening. I was seeking help from all kinds of doctors who were running all kinds of tests. I had been told that my testosterone was low, so I started to receive pellets injected under my skin for assistance with that. In the beginning it helped, but then it would wear off and not help after some time. I then went looking for a new doctor to help me find this missing piece to my puzzle. I knew I was struggling with something but couldn't explain it all. After tons of testing and doctor visits and thousands of dollars later, I myself had an epiphany. I realized I knew the answer to the question. Why was I feeling so empty, tired, lost, and stressed?

Why do you think it was? What is your hypothesis? What had I not been willing to really think about and embrace from what I already knew? Do you know? **All the answers to your life are right inside you.**

I then went to see a hormone specialist, and there were all kinds of problems he found going on in my system. He wanted thousands of dollars to help me. I was still not convinced this was really my problem. I had been to several very expensive doctors, all of whom had numerous reasons why I was struggling and not feeling healthy. I was not convinced by any of them that it was going to take medication to heal me. I was in BELIEF that my body can heal itself. I was seeking and reading and meditating on ways to heal my body without more medication. I had already learned from Dr. Wayne Dyer and Louise Hay that this is possible, thus I was trying to find how I could too. I was in total belief that anything is possible. I was living from a mindset in which I understood that this is my journey, to find healing to help others. I would not stop until I received answers. I was seeking guidance in every which way. I was being told by numerous doctors it would cost me thousands to be healed. I did not have that to put out there in this moment. I was spinning in my mind because I wanted healing as badly as I need air to breathe. I was thirsty for knowledge and the truth of my healing.

This journey continued on for some time, and I was seeking all types of methods to heal my body: power of prayer, plant-based diet, meditation, yoga, sound healing, bone broth cleanse, Isagenix cleanse, and many more modalities I can't even pronounce. I was seeking and seeking and praying and praying for God to bring me the answers.

I started to do something daily that I believed was part of the metamorphosis, the changing from the caterpillar to the butterfly. Metamorphosis is the process of transformation from the immature form to an adult in stages. I was seeking new ways to live, love, and exist. I was believing to achieve whatever I thought possible in this life. I know in the Bible it states that anything is possible, and I truly believed in this. I was seeking how to make that happen. I was reading affirmations daily. One of my favorites was, "I rise in the strength of Spirit; my whole being is uplifted and renewed." (Divine Science Federation International, 2016) I started to feel better slowly, and I was questioning the why and how. I wasn't sure what was kicking in and why I was starting to feel better. I wanted to believe it was because of the power of belief that I was healing my body but how could I be sure?

I started going into deep prayer and thanking God, sometimes hourly, for what He was doing in my life. As I did this, I started to see more signs that everything was coming together, and I was coming out of this fog. I wanted to believe it was God lifting me out of this hell on earth that now, more than once, I was feeling. This was not the first time I was living hell on earth and why was I not allowing God to heal me this time?

I had serious doubt, depression, and darkness come over me daily. It was in those moments that I realized I was becoming this butterfly, but I was not allowing myself to transform. I was holding myself back because I was not shedding my former self and allowing this new beautiful me to rise up out of the ashes of despair or to be released from the cocoon. I was seeking truth and love but sinking back down into the darkness and then coming into the light. It was almost as if I was making breakthroughs and then sinking back down into self-doubt. Then I would rise up and try to spread my wings and fall back down in despair.

One of the movies that I love for all times is *ROCKY*. I love this movie because Rocky falls and fails over and over and then continues to rise up. He seeks growth and freedom through the journey. People, this is our lives. It hit me like a ton of bricks. We are constantly changing, falling, and getting back up. It is in those moments that we are learning and living. We are growing and thriving. We are BECOMING who we are meant to BE! We are here for a short time to BECOME who we are meant to BE. That is the plan. We are to learn, experience, love, grow, become, be, and move on.

If we can look at life through a simple lens, then we can understand from a place of peace. It is all about loving each other, living each moment to the fullest, and BECOMING the beautiful butterfly you are meant to be. This is it. Why do we make everything so difficult? The Bible tells us in Galatians 5:16, "Walk in the Spirit, and you shall not fulfill the lust of the flesh." The flesh is our negative minds going on and on, circling us and ruminating in fear and worries, allowing us to believe we are not worthy or capable of the goodness of God.

How to Metamorphose (transform from the immature stages of life into the mature stages of life.)

1. Believe in Faith. (Believe in the power of prayer. Say to yourself, "God I want to see your power in my life daily.")
2. Speak in Faith. (Speak as if God has already completed the miracle you are praying about.)
3. Act in Faith. (Know God is guiding your path. Take action knowing your prayers have been answered.)

My dear butterfly, it is time for you to spread your beautiful wings and fly. It is time for you to let go of the fear, which is false evidence appearing real; believe in who you are meant to be, ditch the self-doubt, and BECOME the best version of you. The time spent in the cocoon is meant to change you, to mature you, and then you are to deal with the struggle and learn to fly. This is life. We are born as the caterpillar. Then we deal with the happenings of life and mature and grow. We each go into transformation at some time in our life and we struggle to become that beautiful being who can fly, who can soar above the clouds.

When I was searching for help in my transformation, I was working with a shaman who does energy healing. This experience helped my transformation. She could help me understand the struggle I had been dealing with all my life and assist me in releasing it. In this journey, people will come into your life to help you climb the mountain and to help you get to that next step on your path. It is in these moments, when you search for change and you thirst for knowledge, that your transformation is happening. Your wings are growing, and your old self is shedding.

You are unique, beautiful, and unstoppable. It is time to believe that and take action in pursuit of your dreams, desires, and visions. You have a dream planted in your soul to become, and now is the time to believe that anything is possible.

Thank you for spending this quality time with me, my dear friend. I want the world for you, and I want you to know you are loved, unique, and amazing. You are meant to flourish and fly! Today, start your journey to being in love with who you are and living your life to the fullest. Don't wait to have the millions, perfect health, or career that you are longing for. It will all come when you believe in power. You have the power and you can choose to love this life. Just start today, my friend. In peace and love, go accomplish your dreams and fly to new heights, you beautiful butterfly!

During these years, I was diagnosed with PTSD (post-traumatic stress disorder), generalized anxiety, Bipolar Disorder, and hormonal deficiencies. I truly do believe many of these situations are because of the negative place my mind had been functioning from. I am daily renewing my mind and transforming my life, seeking and finding ways to be in love with this life, believing and having faith to be an overcomer one day at a time, living in the moment and finding peace, renewing my mind and becoming who I am meant to be in Christ! Daily I'm repeating to my mind, "I am spirit. The kingdom of God lives in me and I am peace, love, joy, harmony, and I am powerful. I am perfect health."

I am sharing this to help others be released from their prisons in their minds. If this helps transform one individual, that is a celebration of life!

Today BECOME who you are meant to BE! Love this Life.

“We delight in the beauty of the butterfly, but rarely admit the changes it has gone through to achieve that beauty.”

~ Maya Angelou

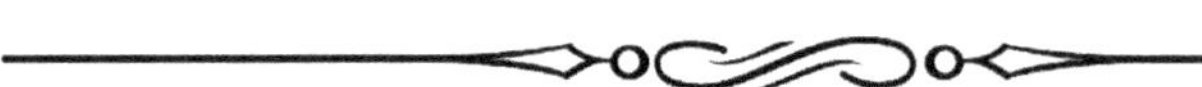

CHAPTER 7

The Discovery Of Gemma

By Gemma Castiglia

I would like to introduce myself. My name is Gemma (Marie) Castiglia and I am 49 years of age. I thank you from the bottom of my heart for reading my condensed, short story. I am honored, humbled, and super proud of whom I've transformed into on my Holistic Life Journey.

I will upfront warn you, my story will possibly 'metaphorically' feel like a mix/minestrone of my life.

However, I hope by the end you will feel the raw and real depth of my life journey up to now and my passion and pure, heartfelt love for my mom, my dad, and myself.
I was 11 years old when my mother Maria passed away suddenly in our family home in Campbellfield Northern Suburbs, Melbourne Victoria, Australia.

Prior to this day, what I do remember adding to my father's recollection was that we were a happy, humble Italian family whose parents migrated in the mid-1950's to Australia. My parents were from the same village in Italy, Abruzzo. They met, fell in love, got married, and migrated to Australia in the 1950's, leaving the post-World War II suffering and anguish behind like many immigrants of that time, sacrificing in courage and bravery into the unknown for a happier, free life for themselves and their family.

I was two when we moved to Campbellfield from North Fitzroy. My parents' vision was for a new home (land and package style) with a toilet inside and a decent size garage for dad's Kingwoods and mom's love for parties and entertaining (which I inherited the entertaining, not the Kingwoods).

My dad was a very hard worker and quite domesticated, and he would help my mom around the kitchen and home. He was also a farmer from his upbringing in Italy, so his garden, huge herb, vegie patch and flowers, especially the roses, was up there with his true loves. I was the youngest of three, the baby of the family, and as there was a big age gap between us, I jokingly called myself the love child to my father.

This is now where it's gest kinder all mixed up and interesting.

If you were to ask me what the journey lowlights and highlights were, or which has had the strongest impact and significance and brought the biggest life lessons, growth and wisdom, I would have to say it was my mother's sudden, tragic death.

My mom had a massive heart attack and stroke two days after her 52nd birthday on the eighth of July, 1980. It was a cold, winter's Tuesday night in Melbourne. (Keep in mind, this is my recollection, although after my momma's death, I blocked a big chunk of my life prior and was later labeled with PTSD.)

My folks had picked me up from school, St Matthews Catholic Primary School. My mother was not feeling well. She had been to the doctor, was told she had flu symptoms and that she should go home and rest. I was in grade six and had a school excursion the next day and went to bed early that evening. I remember being awakened around 10.30pm that evening from the phone ringing and shouting and loud screams from people in our home.

A neighbor came into my room, and as she opened the door, I saw my mother lying flat on the carpet in front of the gas heater. I remember saying out loud "Mom is dead" not understanding as an 11 year-old what that exactly meant. All I could hear were the shouts and screams and ambulance sirens. This was extremely traumatic for me as a young girl, and 1980 was a totally different world to now. I remember having vivid dreams after mom passing, that the ambulance took her away but she was still alive; later learning with my education and training that this was a part of my feelings of abandonment and shock.

I was taken to a sibling's house nearby and was up most of the night with neighbors, family friends, and relatives. I had no idea what was really happening and how much this night would regress and severely impact my life.

In the early hours of the morning, I was taken back to my home. I was instructed to go to my momma, whom had now been deceased for over eight hours.

"To kiss her goodbye, to be strong and not to cry".

Let me set the scene for you. My father and other family members were medicated and in shock. The room was filled with people in dark black attire holding rosary beads. It was a heavy, scary experience. My closest friends who were my age could not walk into that room for years after.

Unbeknown to me at that time, I was an old, gifted soul. My courageous, brave, responsible self walked in and did as I was told. I said goodbye and kissed my angelic mom.

May she eternally REST IN PEACE.

My adolescent and teen years were quite tough for me and my daddy. Believe it or not, to those who knew me, I was a quiet child. However, my third eye vision, attention to detail and people's energies were huge. I hung out with the cool kids, regardless. I had this uncanny gift to see and sift energy. I used to hide under my parents' bed when certain people came to our home; especially males with facial hair and beards; and being in the 70s, this was fashionable and abundant. However, they assumed I was scared of the facial hair, not that I could see through them energetically.

Two years after mom passed, my dad almost remarried. His priority and concern was me being a child and needing a mother to raise and nurture me unconditionally. My daddy was also an old soul and had a huge spiritual intent and third eye. This allowed him to be much more open to life.

I was a light worker, so my dad and I connected spiritually the most. This led to lots of jealousy, envy, and manipulation by those around us. We were unaware of it until I was much older. When future events unfolded with the family, we realized that we both had so much negativity and energetic and spiritual attack on and around us.

Energy, Good or Bad, Unconscious or Conscious, Does Exist and Manifest.

I found out later in life that I had an old soul, rebellious side to me. Thank goodness!

I lived a life where I fell into being "older young" I looked "older younger" and as I journeyed to heal myself and evolve as I got older, I started to actually look younger. It was like my inner child spirit-self became more youthful, self-nurturing and healing with age.

I was a lost little girl, running around town go-getting and living two lives, in a way. I did what most teens did, I partied, experimented and suppressed my deep pain and loss. I needed and longed for my mom and was emotionally and mentally stuck, broken, and consciously unaware. My teens were the years that I gave my dad lots of grief, just as many other teens did.

I didn't like school, as I found main-stream academia boring. I had a deep yearning to help and guide people and pass on information with my intuitive gifts; however, there were lots of people around me who were envious, jealous, negative and controlling, and who did their best to shut me down energetically, and who did everything they could to "keep baby silent' and keep the spotlight on themselves.

Luckily, the universe stepped in and my daddy and I did awaken to it with the help of my momma in heaven; however, this part of my life happened later, so I hope you keep reading.

No one had explained death to me, nor did they think to advise me that my mom had a heart condition and hypertension and that there was nothing that could be done for her. My dad was trying so hard to keep it all together and raise me as best he could with (undiagnosed) depression onsets and mood swings. The poor man worked two jobs and long hours to bring me up, educate me, and give me as much as a single parent doing it alone could. Family around him were in victim vibration, raising their families and, like many others of that era, focused on materialism and wealth and control over their environment and everyone in it.

At the age of 15, life got the better of me. 'I needed my mom'. My friends around me were a combination of nice and mean girls and bullies, who were also loaded with jealousy and envy.

At 16, I was suicidal. I had had enough of the voices which I thought at the time were inside my head, and I had no understanding or education to assist me about my esoteric gifts or open third eye till later in life. I just didn't want to be on this earth anymore. I was exhausted and I felt like I rushed back into this life to save my dad and to be with him and to experience the mother and father healing that followed.

I vividly remember sitting in the bathroom, holding a razor blade, ready to end my life and the deep anguish and emotional grief, loss, and pain. But the thought of leaving my daddy alone with all the sacrifices he made for me and the family; I just couldn't do it to him. I remember the loneliness, the sobbing, the sadness, the deep anguish and pain; however, for my daddy, I put on a brave face and got on with it.

Leading into my early 20's, I became quite the party girl and I managed to unconsciously balance two lives, even whilst lots of people did their darn hardest to stop this from occurring. They did not like the fact that I had some freedom and a life they felt they missed out on, due to the decade in which they were born. The little girl soldier/fighter in me fought the fight, whilst people closest to us tried to turn my dad and I against each other, but it didn't work. My dad and I stuck together like two musketeers. Our unconditional love was too strong to be broken.

In 1994, after being bridesmaid and maid of honor seven times, I decided to finally go overseas to Italy and Europe by myself for two and a half months, which my daddy wasn't happy about/me traveling alone. My daddy was an old school task master. I had to be an adult first, then teenager/young adult. Plus, he had to worry as parents do, all alone as a sole parent.

I was 25, and most of my friends were getting engaged and married, as that's what the girls of that generation did at the time. For me...well, my life was different.

I was already metaphorically a 'house wifey'. I was looking after a man, cleaning, cooking, running a household with dad, under pressure and expectations plus. Dad retired and was on the pension and I knew then that I needed to do more, so that as he got older, I could help him as the role-reversal unfolded. It was just my turn. He had cared for me, and now my journey to care for him more was commencing.

Of course I wanted to meet someone and fall in love. I am a romantic old soul. However, my folks married in their late 20's back in the 50's so I figured I had time. (After my trip to Italy, I almost got engaged to a wonderful man; however, we ended up breaking up and he ended up marrying his first love whom he met during high school).

During this time in my mid 20's, I wanted to adventure, explore, work, travel and succeed so that when I did meet my life partner, I was ready wiser and so that Dad and I could live a more comfortable life and not worry about having to go without to live.

Others didn't necessarily see what happened behind closed doors, but it wasn't any of their business anyway. Plus, firstly and mostly, they would also have needed to face the hard up truth of what they themselves were not doing, not what they pretended to be.

So I planned this huge trip to Europe and it was the beginning of an exciting new journey for me. I left in July with ALITALIA, who flew from Melbourne to Rome back in those days. It was hard leaving my dad alone. He was fit and healthy, but I knew he would be alone lots and I was right. I would call my besties at the time, who would inform me that hardly anyone visited him while I was away. My Dad was a soldier/trooper and got on with it, as deep down, he knew this was something I had to do.

It was my first big trip of my life and the start of my love for overseas and love for travel. I have so many stories and occurrences which commenced the conscious awareness and opening of my light working, mediumship, psychic and holistic healer journey.

I may have left Australia on my own, however in the months that I traveled, I was literally only alone for three days. It was like leaving Australia had awakened and reignited my gifts, and my angelic mother traveled with me to guide and protect me and assist in re-opening my gifts and channel so I could totally connect with her in Italy, the country she and dad were born and raised in. I could connect to our strong ancestry, including my mom's mom, my grandmother Gemma. Traveling alone was rewarding, challenging, and at times, risky and dangerous...especially with this expansive auric energy field and light I had, but was not fully aware of.

I now believe negativity and darkness is very drawn to the light, like insects and moths are drawn to light. I started this realization that jealous, envious evil manipulative beings would be drawn to me like flies and manifest energetically. This commenced my increasing curiosity of the spiritual world. With mom in heaven, I was the chosen brave one drawn and guided to readers at a youngish age, at a time very different to now, where so many are 'supposedly spiritual'.

I was an innocent, somewhat naïve girl at the time, who just wanted to connect with mom, and to make sure that she was ok. I would go home and pass on messages to dad and reassure him that she was ok.

You see, as humans, we know that losing loved ones is so painful. What some didn't acknowledge was the person who has passed. How my mom missed out on so many years on Earth with family, the love of her life, her husband, and her baby girl growing up from age 11 without her, and not to be here to nurture, guide and protect, me.

As my awareness grew and opened in my life journey, I felt so much more energetically connected to Mom. My ancestors in the spirit world helped me realize my mom did what she had to do to connect with me and raise me up from heaven.

In Italy, I got to visit where my parents grew up and eventually met. I got to know my family there for the first time and to connect with my uncle, who lived in Rome and who was like a father to my mom and helped her get on the boat to leave Italy to be with my dad and start a new life in Australia. I also visited their houses and the cemetery where my grandparents were buried. My uncle made me speak proper Italian (not dialect) which later in life, with all my Italian studies and my trip to Italy, paved the way for me to learn my second fluent language and build a love of languages.

I was also able to experience intimacy on another level in Florence, Italy. In Australia, with the knowing that my mother was watching me, it was more difficult, as she was a strict, devout catholic. I knew my mother would have wanted me to wait for 'the one'. I also knew then that this could be years away. So, without getting more personally into it, this trip was monumental and life-changing for many reasons and it opened my future world to energy and spirituality; the positives, the negatives, the unknowns, people's true agendas...the good, the bad and the ugly. I had to come to terms with so much: the loss of my mother, my strong emotional tie to my father, my suicidal, emotional thoughts. The lost little girl running around town, not being allowed to integrate life, be a kid and an adult...not knowing how to slow down and not having the support of nurturing females. I was so lucky to have my mother around me, guiding me from heaven, and my beautiful, loyal father who is also 'a little girl's first love'. He was the most loving (in his own way) and supportive father a girl could ever ask for.

Post Italy, my intuition opened rapidly as did my esoteric, psychic and mediumship spiritual awareness gifts and spiritual connection. Messages I had blocked back as a teen had resurfaced again, prepping me with what was to come.

Almost 22 years of education, learnings, teachings and experiences brought me to places unimaginable to me, and sparked the start of a love affair with the world, in particular the USA.

I had the realization that I had to heal the hurt and all the emotions that were deeply suppressed and connected to the loss of my mother as well as the deep, emotional connection to my father. I knew that if I didn't heal now, I may never fully recover when he crossed over to be with my mother. My reconnection to spirituality, Jesus, God and healing all my health issues that all stemmed from deep emotional trauma, emotional, mental stress and anxiety. Rebalancing and reintegrating myself and working through my inner self, to heal both my inner and outer self and reconnect with the creator and the angelic realm.

A few years after returning from Italy, a friend of mine who was involved with Landmark Education and who knew my history and the fact that I had little pre-memory of mom passing, called me up one night and suggested I do a weekend forum with Landmark and suggested it could help me unblock the memories which were post trauma. I was on the journey to heal all this and heal myself and my health issues that stemmed from her passing. I was always a very energetic and open person and I was on a mission to heal myself. I was following my inner guidance with the assistance of my angelic mother around me, wanting to synchronize all the monumental events in my life into a healing timeline to uncover and clear all my life blocks.

So I attended the forum in Melbourne and it significantly changed my life and started another road map on my path to heal. Landmark did open me to vulnerability; however, it also paved the way to me discovering my life path and what I was born to do. It led me to Reiki Energy Healing and Massage Therapy, which led me to my dream and passion of being a sole trader and self-employment. I was informed by the Reiki master that I had healing hands and I had come into this life to use this gift to help and heal others.

This sparked that deep inner calling to heal and help as many people as possible, especially those who, like myself, had lost a parent or their childhood and innocence at a young age. I completed my first Reiki course and two certificates in massage therapy and continued up from there. I built up a business on energy healing and massage bodyworks therapy and started with mobile services and home clinic. I left my full-time job and worked part-time for a while, then moved fully into my business in 2006.

A big part of wanting to be self-employed and be my own boss was also my dad. I knew I was going to be the one full-time caring for him, while others would only step in at the end (and try and claim most of the credit).

I also really wanted my own family and children but didn't want a child or to marry just for the sake of it.

I did have two Divine opportunities throughout my life to be a mother impregnating in my late 20's and again in my mid 40's, but the universe had other plans for me. I realized more and more with all my life hardships and lessons that I was born to heal, both myself as well as others...this was my Divine mission.

In August 2006, I was 36 years of age and in mid-life, or as some of you may know, Pluto square. We had a big family feud. This event totally erupted and changed both my life and my daddy's life, and life as we knew it would never be the same again. We spent a full-on year being harassed, bullied, dealing with restraining orders, so much bullshit and bitterness and the unveiling of the past truths. We were coming to terms with what was being conjured up behind closed doors for year's prior: the power/control/birth rights and master manipulation that surrounded us with the possibility of losing our home and being thrown out on the streets.

My father and I had to unite more than ever, and with the sheer, resilient, authentic, supportive and professional people around us. We fought, the two of us. The universe totally supported us and we won the battle to keep our home. We did however have to resign to the fact that those around us were conditional, victims, and to a point, narcissistic in behavior. We, in our belief and value system, stuck to the truth and followed our instincts, intuition and our hearts. As sad as parts of the outcome was, we got to see the truth, and as the saying goes, "Those who live in the truth sleep well and peaceful through the night".

This experience was tough and it gave my dad and I a chance to uncover so many truths, learn and grow from it, heal and support each other to the bittersweet end. From that day, we no longer had a relationship with them and had to accept this, as everything does happen for a reason, bad or good, and God would never allow this to happen if it wasn't Divinely ordered.

Post family supreme court actioned feud, in 2008, my beautiful daddy started experiencing symptoms of confusion and lethargy. A year later, a few days after a doctor's visit with these symptoms and other symptoms, he was misdiagnosed with severe rheumatism. Dad had a massive fall at home in the back yard and collapsed on the concrete fall. I took him to the 24-hour clinic in Mill park, and there, he had his second fall, which put him in a coma.

He was rushed to the Epping Northern Hospital where he was in emergency and ICU for a week, then in a ward for weeks and rehab for over a month. I remember like it was yesterday, the day dad was admitted into ICU when the doctors called an emergency meeting and I was asked if dad and I had discussed turning off life support, as he had Type 2 Respiratory Lung Failure and was a carbon dioxide retainer. Basically, dad wasn't breathing out effectively, which meant his body was filled with carbon dioxide poison. This was the first we had heard of this diagnosis after a year of trying to figure out what was wrong with him and misdiagnosed, not to mention the decade plus prior, where he was twice misdiagnosed with Parkinson's but actually had a longstanding nervous tremor.

Of course I was in total shock, tears flowed, as this was the first time I had been given all this info and was informed I had 24 to 48 hours to decide to turn the machine off which was keeping him alive. To add to it, it was two days before his 83rd birthday, October 27. I had very good friends with me, but ultimately, I was his daughter and medical power of attorney and had to make the decision, and honestly, I was broken!

You now understand, my dad and I, with everything we had endured and conquered, were not just father and daughter. We were soulful best friends and each other's reasons for living and we only had each other. Our relationship was rare and the love was soulfully powerful. He truly had my back, and he didn't like confrontation. When he did have to stand up to injustice, harassment and bullying, he rose to the challenge. I was a mirror image of him at times, with my mother's guidance and support.

A few days after being told this news and keeping dad on life support, dad miraculously woke up just in time for his birthday and his first words to me were "Where's my birthday cake?" as he did love his sweets. Not long after, dad slowly regained his appetite. He had also broken his leg, so he had to be admitted to the wards to monitor his lung disease and heal his leg. He was then admitted to rehab, where he recovered and healed his leg well and made some lifelong friends. He was a humble man and people just liked being around his humble energy.

Following this few couple of month's ordeal, dad came home and I had to continue to care for him as his leg was still in plaster. That is unconditional love! I worked part-time and became his full-time home carer. His leg healed, but unfortunately his respiratory disease didn't, and we spent the next five years in and out of hospital and dad was on a full-time oxygen tank.

Dad only had me and he was my dad. Looking after him was an honor, as difficult as it was at times.

With everything that had transpired, I knew I was the one who loved him unconditionally and the one who was going to care for him regardless, and the one he entrusted. Dad and I were now out of denial and fully aware of the facts and the truth.

Three years into caring for dad solely at home, it took a toll on my own health and I knew I had to holistically look after myself as well. If something happened to me, who would look after him? I started with yearly admittance for dad to respite and I would take a break and most of the time go overseas where I healed the best.

I rediscovered my love for travel in the country where I resonated the most and my soul felt like it was home: America. From 2012, I started traveling there yearly and had also been advised by a mentor to study and train up as a hypnotherapist, which I did and qualified as a NLP Master Practitioner in Nevada, USA. I continued here in Australia and completed my advanced clinical hypnotherapy and mesmerism training.

My intention was to combine my esoteric spiritual energetic healing and clinical services to guide, assist those in need of a total overhaul (like a full car service). Body, mind, heart and life rebalance and reintegration. I knew the path to my healing journey and how I could help and heal others to possibly not endure life the way I had to.

A few years later, dad got worse; he needed more care including night respiration monitoring, plus it started becoming a little dangerous leaving him alone when I had to go do shopping, get meds, etc. He was now on full-time oxygen. I had no choice...I was medically and professionally advised to put him in full-time nursing care.

The first year was the hardest. He wanted to be in his home and to add, he wasn't getting the care he needed and I was there daily providing extra fresh food and his favorites, including donuts and KFC, DVDs and his love for western movies, history and religious movies, and his love for opera and classical music. I took him out on outings, and when I needed a break, I had an amazing support system to step in. Dad continued going to his activity group and they would pick him up three times a week, and he made lots of friends and spent his last ten years living and enjoying his life after the years of sacrifice he gave to his family.

I was blessed with a unique relationship with my father and I am so proud of him. We fought the fight.

We stayed as humble and integral as possible, and we were lucky to have such open spiritual awareness and understanding, and the love we had for each other stood the test of so many lifetimes.

Daddy Antonio's journey became popular on FB and he privately loved the attention. He didn't understand how social media worked, but he loved me reading him the posts and looking at all the photos. During the toughest of times, the posts of prayers and kind words of support made it all the more bearable for the both of us.

Dad lost his battle to Respiratory Lung Disease and passed away January 3rd, 2016 with kidney failure, due to the meds for fluid retention due to the disease. That was the toughest day of my adult life, and I have never felt so much pain and anguish by his side to the end. The last look he gave me before he closed his eyes for the last time was a look a father gives an eight year old daughter.

As we all know, in our parent's eyes, we are always their child, first and forever.

With all I had endured and missed out on my journey, from losing my mom and the long road to heal my inner self, I vowed I would heal my relationship with my dad whilst he was alive and tell him often how blessed and honored I was to be his daughter and that he was the best father a girl could ever ask for.

He was my world and I miss him every single day.

"Daddy, we made it through together till the bittersweet end. You will be always and forever in my heart."

I'll finish up with this as I sit here in heartfelt tears...

Three weeks after dad's passing, I had a dream of him. He told me to move to Mooloolaba (which is close by to Alexandra Headland). I had no idea where this location was, as I had never been to the Sunshine Coast of Queensland. I started researching and flew up. As soon as my feet hit the ground, I knew this was going to be my 'Eat Love Pray' mid' part of my life where I would heal on the deepest level and bring myself to my next evolution of life and healing myself.

I honored the promise I had made to not sell the family home till after he passed. A year later, I sold up in Melbourne leaving behind the hardships and living 46 years in the same suburb and home and made the bold, brave, sea change and moved up to the Sunshine Coast Queensland to Alexandra Headland at the Mantra Break Free Resort near the AVALON building (my business name). Huge signs!

I had to come to terms with the fact that I was now truly an orphan and on my own, whilst knowing my mom and dad had finally reunited in heaven, and spent a big chunk of 2017 healing the deepest aspects of myself and my soul; the parts that couldn't heal till I left Melbourne.

I dedicate this opportunity and short story to my beautiful, angelic, selfless parents, Maria and Antonio Castiglia. May they both live in restful peace forever in the light, until we meet again.

I now dedicate myself to my AVALON HEALING SERVICES as earth light worker, medium, psycho-spiritual healer, clearer, counselor, hypnotherapist and transitional and transformational life coach, holistic and clinical therapist.

I assist healing and empowerment with an open, healing heart, those ready to heal and awaken themselves, whom are ready to deeply and courageously move forward to being the best version of themselves and to discover their life purpose and passions and the life they were born to live and their legacy.

I am about to rebrand my business and take it global. My intention is to be able to assist and see clients from anywhere in the world, thanks to the powerful internet, and to continue my life mission and reach out to as many as possible with the knowledge and freedom to do so.

I will continue my journey and be an information bearer and bring out my voice, knowledge and gifts via social media, radio and media. I will empower and expose the holistic and spiritual world to as many people who are ready to listen, awaken and action their lives.

I am also ready to meet my soul mate and life partner, and I am prepared to move heaven and Earth for him and combine my love for him, travel and adventure, whilst building our empires and life together.

Thank you for taking the time to read my story. It has been extremely tough, as I recently lost a friend to suicide. This has added to me to dig deep to what I needed to share with you, and I truly hope the parts of my journey and story that I shared resonates, touches and empowers you and your life.

"WE HAVE ONE CHANCE AT THIS LIFE AS WE KNOW IT AND WE DESERVE TO LIVE AND LOVE IT TO THE

ABSOLUTE FULLEST"

"Truly, the greatest gift you have to give, is that of your own self-transformation."

~ Lao Tzu

CHAPTER 8

Always in Control

By Liz Palmer

The Preachers Kid (PK)

There are many things in life that define us as we grow up. I had a normal childhood, the youngest of five children, and my father was a Lutheran Minister. My mom was a housewife and she had her hands full with all of us, and her duties as a preacher's wife. When I was five, we moved from Atlanta, Georgia, to Tucson, Arizona, and most of my memories begin there. Our family life revolved around the church, but I had plenty of time to play and be a normal kid. So what happened to make me strive for certainty and control in my adult life?

I attended a small parochial school through seventh grade and my mom kept us all busy with piano lessons and swim team practice. There was a great neighborhood gang consisting of three sets of sisters plus my next-door neighbor. We were all within two years of age of each other and spent a lot of time at each other's houses well into high school. My mom was loving and resilient and, like her mother, was a very strong woman. She did have one fault, though: she was always late! So, guess what? I'm the most punctual person in the world. My dad was very learned and very reserved, a hands-off parent, but that was the norm back then. He would let me give him back rubs and comb his hair into funny styles, which I loved to do. It was great fun growing up with four siblings (three sisters and one brother). We were all born two years apart, so it was me, my sister, my brother in the middle, and two older sisters. My sister closest to my age was my best friend. My brother tortured us all, and as I grew older I got closer to my two older sisters.

Let me describe the PK part of my life. Of course, we had to go to church every Sunday, which was kind of fun as my father preached at the university campus church, except for the times when we were part of the service. We were called upon to sing, read the Bible, and sometimes perform skits. I was extremely shy, so this was torture for me. We had an altar in the house and were expected to pray every morning when we woke up. We did do normal things like camping in San Diego for two weeks every summer, but we would also have a family service on Sundays at our campsite. As a PK, we all had to set a good example; misbehaving was not an option. As I grew older, I did resent the infringement on my time for doing my PK duties, but I now realize the profound effect it had on me. I am an extremely spiritual person and have a strong belief in a higher being, and that brings a lot of of calm and peace into my daily life.

Cancer Strikes

On the last day of seventh grade I came home and my mom told me that my dad had been diagnosed with cancer. He was in and out of remission for two years and died when I was 15. During those two years we navigated through his illness and what it entailed, none of it pleasant. I suddenly found that the supervisory iron grip on me had been loosened, as my father was the disciplinarian and my mom was busy taking care of my dad. On the one hand, I didn't want to upset my dad, but he was too sick to keep track of what I was doing. Towards the end of eighth grade, I started experimenting with alcohol and a few other substances and so began what were to be my wildest years (High School). Compared to most, it wasn't wild at all, but it was a time when I wasn't driven by certainty. Despite my dabbling, I was still responsible, did extracurricular activities, had a boyfriend and a part-time job. I loved choir class and qualified for a small group called the Troubadours during my junior year. Looking back, I see that both our amazing choir conductor and the camaraderie in the choir was a grounding force for me. But I was also the first to change out of my cheerleading uniform and hop into someone's four-wheel drive for a boony party on Friday nights. After my dad died, I was bitter (how could someone who served God die?) and lost my faith a bit. It took a few years for all this to settle and for me to realize what I needed to do.

My Quest for Certainty Begins

By the time I was headed for college I had one primary goal, to get a good paying job when I graduated. My mom had had very little work experience when my dad died, and at times I sensed their marriage was not making either of them happy, but she was financially dependent. I vowed to never be financially dependent on anyone EVER. At the time, I didn't connect this need for independence and control with the death of my dad, but I clearly see that now. I was laser focused. The problem was that I didn't have a clue what I wanted to be, so I was a liberal arts undecided major. I did what any motivated but clueless 18-year-old would do and interrogated the successful parents of my dorm hall mates when they came to visit. What did they do? What was the most important skill they needed to be successful? Two business owners each said that finance was the most important skill to successfully run a business. Following their direction, I applied to the school of business and declared my major in accounting, even though I loathed math. I knew I could get a good job when I graduated, and so I suffered through the math. In four and half years, I graduated with a double major (I had to be super sure I could get a job!) in accounting and computer information systems. I studied hard, put myself through college by working part-time and managed to have a lot of fun too!

Out of the Blue

Let's backtrack a bit. Remember when I vowed to never be financially dependent on anyone? That meant that I had zero interest in dating or having a boyfriend. For some crazy reason, I agreed to go on a blind date the summer between my sophomore and junior years. My roommate knew his roommate, and I had briefly met my upcoming date at a bar, so he knew who I was, but because I wasn't interested in guys, I had basically ignored him when he graciously offered me his chair that night in the bar. Boy was I nervous! And now I see that I felt this was a huge loss of control! When the doorbell rang and I opened the door, I saw a kind, handsome, smiling face. I relaxed a bit, and the rest is history. We just celebrated our 32nd wedding anniversary.

After graduating I got a good job with a CPA firm and didn't really like it, but I worked with a great group of people and needed those two years of experience to land a job in the private sector. Meanwhile, five plus years after I met my future husband we got married, but not after we had lived together for two years because I had to be super certain that we would get along. Meeting him was a blessing in disguise because he was my polar opposite. While I planned everything, he was spontaneous. Being married to someone like me would have been really boring. Don't get me wrong, I loved to have fun but my quest for certainty was always lurking in the shadows.

Soon after getting married I got let go from the company I was working for due to the economic downturn. I had just found out that I was pregnant. There was a firestorm going on inside me because: 1) my doctor had advised me that I would have problems conceiving so being pregnant was unexpected, although I was thrilled about it; and 2) who would hire a pregnant woman? This was before maternity leave was common and anti-discrimination rules were nonexistent. I was definitely loosing control. I was a blubbering mess when my hubby pulled into the garage after work. When I told him what had happened, he tried to comfort me and said, "Since you aren't working, why don't we take a drive up the coast of California? I've always wanted to do that." I decided that I could take the want ads with me to look for a job, and off we went! It was a wonderful trip and just what I needed. I got a job soon after returning and did not tell them I was pregnant until after they made me a job offer. Despite my quest for independence and certainty, I had opened up to a relationship that resulted in the creation and birth of our beautiful daughter. This was when my giving nature kicked in. Lo and behold, I did need human interaction to be happy!

On the Move

Another defining moment in my life was when I joined the Foreign Service. I was happily working, married, and raising our daughter. My dear mother-in-law had retired and lived near us. She had joined the Foreign Service in her 40s after her husband died, so I knew it meant working in foreign countries. They were looking for CPAs and, despite having no overseas experience (I had vacationed in Mexico), my mother-in-law claimed I would be a perfect fit. A year and a half after submitting my application, I was off to Washington, D.C., for an interview. I traveled with my mother-in-law and we stayed with a Foreign Service colleague of hers. She was my tour guide and cheerleader before my four-hour interview. It went well and six months later we moved to D.C. for my seven-month training program. My husband and I had both been working in real estate development, which was starting to crash thanks to Charles Keating, best known for his role in the savings and loan scandal of the late 1980s. So we decided to try out the Foreign Service life and take it one assignment at a time. This was definitely a giant leap of faith for me, and one that challenged my desire to be in control, as we had no idea where our first assignment would be.

Little did I know then that my decision would lead to 28 years of working in seven developing countries in Africa, the Caribbean, the Middle East, Southern Asia, and South America. My first assignment was to the Kingdom of Swaziland. Most people asked me, "Where is that?" It is a small country in Southern Africa, which is almost completely surrounded by South Africa, with Mozambique to its east. It is the only African country that consists of one tribe and it has a fascinating history and a king who acquires a new wife every year after the annual reed ceremony. It was also very far away from home and pre-internet, so my husband, daughter, and I bravely packed up our belongings and began our new adventure together. Having culture shock was an understatement! Being surrounded by Swazis scared the crap out of me as I had been bullied in high school, but I soon came to realize how gentle and mellow Swazis were and was fascinated by their culture which can best be described as tribal and African. Imagine going to the grocery store on Saturday morning and being stopped by the police to let a large group of men, wearing only leopard skins and carrying spears, pass through the intersection on their way to a ceremony.

We lived in a small house on Polinjane Road, and I could walk to work down the dirt road to the larger paved street. I really liked my job and loved my new boss who would end up being a friend for life. At work, 85% of the staff were Swazi and I loved working with them. The family was settled into our daily routine and we decided it was time to have another child. One year later and no pregnancy, we decided that our beautiful daughter was enough, but fate had another plan for us. We hosted a Christmas lunch and had a Yankee swap where everyone brought something they didn't really need as a wrapped gift. I ended up with a wooden fertility statue that a friend had gotten as a Peace Corp volunteer in West Africa. I placed it on my nightstand and within a month was pregnant.

Three months later when I traveled to South Africa to see my doctor, I found out we were having twins. I was elated and terrified at the same time. I had had terrible morning sickness and had not gained any weight and I'm a small person to begin with. Thank goodness the sickness abated soon after. We moved into a larger house and I set about trying to find ways to stay in shape so that I would be in prime condition for the delivery. Any sort of organized class soon became impossible due to the size of my stomach, so I would walk home, up this incredibly long and steep road alongside Swazi women carrying everything imaginable on their heads (buckets of water, firewood...). I'm sure they all wondered why this pregnant white woman who surely had a car was walking anywhere. But, as for all things in life, I tended to go after what I wanted when I wanted it with little regard for what others thought. I wanted to be in shape when the twins were born.

All went well until the seventh month when I went into premature labor. My husband drove me to the hospital in South Africa because the one in Swaziland couldn't handle anything complicated. Luckily the labor was stopped and I stayed in South Africa working in our office there, driving to and from work in an ancient Land Rover (like driving a tank), which I swear to this to day is what sent me into labor six weeks later. My husband and daughter would visit on the weekends, but I went into labor during the week, so I begged the hospital to at least let me call my husband before I was whisked into the delivery room. Things went so quickly that the doctor barely got there in time, but I delivered two healthy but small babies, a girl and a boy. Our family was complete. After returning to Swaziland, I looked in the mirror and realized that I was definitely adulting. I was no longer a youngster but someone with immense responsibilities, including three children to raise.

My first assignment brought many changes to my life. I was forced to give up a wee bit of control after the twins, because it was a challenge to work and take care of them. Throughout my career, I felt a little guilty that I couldn't be a full-time mommy. I would have loved that, but I was the one with direct employment and had financial responsibilities. I had also employed two loving Swazi women who took care of our house and family, so it was manageable. I had also finally found my professional calling and loved my job. I worked for an entity that delivered assistance to developing countries. I had found a way to use my financial skills while helping others, and I loved the people I worked with. The bonds I made with the local staff were probably the best part of my job. They were my second family. I mentored them, fought their work battles for them, and was immensely appreciative of the knowledge they had. In this and each assignment after, I made lifelong friends with both my American and local friends, made closer by the incredible experiences we shared. I will be forever grateful to the women who took care of my children as they grew up. We treated them like family and each one cried every time we moved to another country.

Each country we have lived and worked in has been a chapter in our lives, like high school or college, with memories and friends collected along the way. There was the time that my husband and I got certified for scuba diving and stayed in primitive huts with baby twins and brought home a baby green mamba in my carry-on bag. We had incredibly fun TGIF parties on one assignment because there was nowhere else to have fun. The thrill of flying in our little Cessna plane to beaches on the weekend was wonderful. There was the trip to Morocco with a group of friends and all of our kids, where we rented a bus and a tour guide and traveled the country for a week. We relived Indiana Jones at Petra in freezing cold weather. My stay at a remote hotel in northern Pakistan, called Shangrila, was one of the most stunning places I've ever visited. We took frequent trips to Cartagena to soak up the sunshine. Ten years in, my husband got permanently employed, so we decided to continue this life, moving every two to five years and raising third-culture kids.

My Journey Begins

Four countries later, I had a daughter away in college, my husband accepted a one-year assignment in a nearby but dangerous country, and then my second daughter also left for college. It was just me and my son, who had decided to take a gap year, and our dog, Henry. Prior to this, I had been a busy working mother of three that had never given much thought about "me." I ate healthy and exercised in fits and spurts but felt good. For the first time in a very long time I had time to think about what I needed and wanted. I had time! While I missed my husband and daughters, I embarked on a year filled with getting in shape, spending time with friends, and traveling. I hired a personal kick-boxing trainer who whipped me into shape. More importantly I was held accountable to consistently exercise, as I would never miss one of our sessions. I had several groups of amazing friends and started doing things like playing bunko, going to lunch, or just chilling at a friend's house by the pool. I became more spontaneous. When I realized that local holidays would result in a five-day weekend, I asked my son if he wanted to go to Oktoberfest with me and off we went to Munich. Over another long weekend, I flew to Nepal to see two good friends and reconnected with two more who I had fleetingly met in Manila. Looking back now, I realize how much I had missed human connection and "me" time. I was thrilled that I now had that, and, to this day, I carve out time to reconnect with my friends across the globe.

On the work front, I was hoodwinked into becoming a trainer/teacher for the financial management professionals in the agency that I worked for. I was good at what I did, was experienced, and always supported my local staff who were involved in providing training. I would work on the content of the training with them and empower them to go forth and share their knowledge. This group of dedicated trainers asked me to help them develop a Training of Trainers (TOT) class, which, of course, I did. Then they asked me to present the topics that I had developed in the first offering of the course. There were many reasons why I didn't want to do this. I had no formal training in being a trainer and had little-to-no experience training. Plus, I wasn't 100% comfortable being in front of a room of people speaking. Concurrently, I had been asked to deliver a farewell speech on behalf of my colleagues around the world, for our departing CFO at his retirement ceremony. I would be in Washington, D.C. for the TOT class and was the logical choice. What was happening? How was I going to pull this off? I was nervous, to say the least. I literally couldn't breath for my first presentation of the TOT course but had learned a few tricks on how to relax and made it through the presentation. I was also learning a lot about how to prepare for and provide training from the other trainers and used this to help me prepare my speech.

The night before the speech, I was in my hotel room with two colleagues brainstorming the key points I needed to make. I prepared the speech, went to sleep, and practiced the speech with colleagues during a break the next day. The retirement ceremony was during our lunch break. They were somewhat mortified, as I wasn't fully prepared, but they were supportive and infinitely happy that they weren't the ones who were giving the farewell speech. The mantel of responsibility hung heavy over me, as I wanted to represent my colleagues well and wanted to express our gratitude to the CFO, so I practiced that speech nonstop until it was show time.

As I stood before the sea of faces, colleagues that I knew from my work overseas and those who worked in D.C., both in our office and many others, a certain calm came over me. I took a deep breath and launched into my farewell speech, made even more difficult by the emotions running through me and those in the audience, for a man we admired very much. I stuck to the script but spoke from the heart and the words flowed out of me. And thus began my journey of becoming a trainer and speaker. More importantly, I learned two valuable lessons. The first was that to grow you had to challenge yourself to do things outside your comfort zone. The second was that, as a trainer, it took an incredible amount of extra time and energy, but by giving I got way more back from my fellow trainers and students. These two lessons have continued to propel me on my journey.

After recently congratulating my daughter for getting out of her comfort zone and delivering her first speech at a large conference she replied, "I got it from my mama."

All Alone

Some years later while living in country number seven, I found myself living alone for the first time of my life. Having grown up with four siblings and having three children of my own, I had spent my entire life surrounded by family and the occasional family pet. My children were grown and had all graduated from college when my husband reached mandatory retirement age. He was ready to embark on his dream of building a house for us, so he moved back to the USA. I'm an introvert so had no issue about being alone, but it was a bit lonely.

I spent the first six months pampering myself and planning fun vacations to see my husband and then went to the USA for two months' leave. It was wonderful to be able to spend loads of time with family and friends, but being on vacation mode for that long reared its ugly head. Towards the end of my vacation I had a routine doctor appointment and imagine my horror when I stepped on the scale and weighed more than I ever had in my life. Right about that time a friend shared her success using a super food nutritional program and I immediately bought a 30-day supply of the products for my husband, eldest daughter and myself. One extra checked suitcase later and back in country number seven, the three of us started the 30-day system together. So now I was living alone, couldn't drink coffee, drink wine, or eat dairy, but I was dedicated to putting good nutrition in my body and hoped it would take a few pounds off. Little did I know how this one decision would open a whole new world for me.

The system worked and I felt great. I hired a personal trainer and started working out over lunchtime every day at work instead of working through lunch. I had long- term fitness goals and gave myself two years to reach them. Two and half years later I am still consistently working out four to six times a week. I've also lost and kept off 20 pounds and have reduced my body fat by 35%! The key to my success was the amazing products and the support received from a Facebook group that my enrolling sponsor added me to. I was learning so much about nutrition and how important exercise was for health, which was a huge motivator for me. One thing I wasn't expecting was the incredible passion the members of the Facebook group (my tribe) had for personal development. I was mastering the health and fitness part, but what did I need to learn to be a better person on the inside, one who accepted herself, and who could motivate and inspire others? How could I get comfortable sharing the products that had so positively affected my life with others? How could I trust in the universe when I only trusted myself?

I recently took a short quiz offered by Tony Robbins to determine what my driving force was and, of course, my driving force was certainty. My powers are consistency, trustworthiness, completion of tasks, faith in a higher power, and organization. That is me to a tee! When I recently asked Facebook friends to post a GIF that makes them think about me I got posts like "don't stop, don't give up" and "just keep going." So, along with my need for certainty, I also had fortitude and determination on my side and set out to start broadening my horizons through personal development. I lived in a different country than my tribe, so I took advantage of online courses, team zoom calls, audible books, and remote book clubs. When I was in the USA, I think my husband got a bit perplexed as I was frequently on my computer when he got home, listening, talking, and learning with different groups of people on a variety of subjects.

I started learning about network marketing and how to communicate and connect with others. I signed up for a course called *The Four Colors of Influence* by Growth-U and learned how to communicate with others based on what motivates them. I learned that connecting is a skill, as not everyone communicates as you do. You need to understand who you are communicating with and, above all, to believe in yourself. While I'm not a dedicated network marketer yet, I was learning many valuable lessons I could use in my daily life. I started learning about wealth creation and what the flaws were in my money mindset.

I joined a remote book club for the book *Secrets of the Millionaire Mind* by T. Harv Eker. Every week we met online and would discuss what we had read and how that translated into how we handled money. It was a small group, so we were very honest with each other and quickly realized where our money mindsets were flawed and why. My flaw was that I never felt like I had enough money, so I just worked harder and harder to get more. This was not true. I had been resisting my husband's dream of building a retirement home for us, because I knew it would cost a bloody fortune. He has the most impeccable taste and only the best would do. My approach was that it would cost too much and I had worked hard all my life and didn't want to be beholden to a house. His approach was that this was his dream that we had been planning for many years. He was going to put his heart and soul into the project and it would be wonderful. It would all work out. At some point, I realized that he had to live his dream and I would benefit from having an amazing house to live in. My negativity about the financing of the house was not doing anyone any good. We met with our financial planner who assured us that we could afford this. I had to be certain, and now I vowed to stop resisting and start embracing this project. The house is nearing completion and it is a work of art, a haven for me to return to when I move back to the USA, a place where we can share the best of times with our family and friends.

By reading *The Five Love Languages* by Gary Chapmen, I learned that my love language was acts of kindness. I truly appreciated it when someone did something that lightened my load. I shared this with my family and encouraged them to read the book, as I wanted to know what their love languages were. I learned about the power of intention—what you think you become—and how important it is to envision all of the details of where you want to be, what you want to achieve. I created a vision board that I look at constantly. It contains my financial goals and all things that are important to me. As I learn and grow, my vision is constantly changing, so it's time to update! Daily affirmations and gratitude are now a part of my daily life. You have to be thankful for what you have in order to attract more. I am definitely a glass-half-full person, but when doubts and negativity start bouncing around in my brain, I now know how to shut that down. John Gordon states in *The Carpenter* that, "Negative thoughts are the nails that build a prison of failure. Positive thoughts will build you a masterpiece."

All of what I had learned coalesced last summer when I was in Washington, D.C., for work. I listened to *The Universe Has Your Back: Transform Your Fear into Faith* by Gabriel Bernstein every day to and from work on the Metro. I vowed to live a life of love and joy. Anything else didn't serve me. I learned about the power of meditation, and started doing yoga to have time to contemplate. I learned that my presence is my power. Who I am can have a profound effect on others. To reinforce positivity and the things I was learning I started posting inspirational quotes and information about my journey on social media. I also realized that enjoying the journey was half the fun and to not always be obsessed with the destination. I'm trying to live more in the moment, to embrace and enjoy people and things that I'm attracting, and have realized how fulfilled and happy increased human connection makes me, which brings me to where I am today.

The Future?

I recently started listening to *The Motivation Manifesto: 9 Declarations to Claim Your Personal Power* by Brendon Buchard, which is reinforcing what I'm striving for: choicetime freedom, financial freedom, and spiritual freedom. I'll be retiring in a few years, and so I have time to figure out what the next chapter of my life will look like, but I have a lot of work to do on myself before I get there. Throughout my life, I have always worked hard and at times have resented that I had to do so. I was in constant give mode and sensed that I wasn't getting as much back. What I wasn't doing was opening up myself to receive back. That's changing.

Here's my typical work day. I'm up early and go to the gym. While I'm getting ready for work I listen to an audiobook for a book club I belong to. I work for eight to ten hours, and my job is challenging. Two days a week, I take German class during lunch, and at night and on weekends I have a list of things to do which are either moving me towards my goals or are things that are required of me, like doing my taxes. I'm booked solid, but I'm scheduling my spare time now so that I'm ready for retirement and choicetime freedom. I'm searching for the ways and means that will enable me to give back more when I have that freedom, because I know I will receive back tenfold that which I give to others. I am ready to receive! I want to inspire and motivate people and am practicing doing that now. I reached out to friends to get feedback on whether I was doing so, and one friend said, "Just watching you inspires me: the way you behave, your smiling face, your motivating comments for others, showing concern, and lifting weak spirits." Another commented that my positive energy keeps her inspired. It's working, but I want to amplify this by a thousand.

I want to connect more with my children. Rumor has it that I've been referred to as the Ice Queen. That stung. I am a very loving and caring person but since I was independent and self-sufficient as a young adult, I assumed my children were, too. I didn't want to meddle or be overbearing and I lived very far from them. I was also caught up in my quest for certainty. As I have opened myself up more to others and to them, I have realized that they did need me desperately. They have baggage from being third culture kids (TCK). The frequent moves and resulting sense of loss each time has profoundly affected them. My eldest daughter is on her own personal journey and has been sharing with me how being a TCK has affected her.

Meanwhile I've been obsessed with saving up for and buying my retirement car. I may still get that car but it's not important anymore. My family is. After my trip home for Christmas this year, I knew I had to spend more time with them, and I wasn't scheduled to go home until August and then only for a long weekend. I quickly inquired if my daughters could come home for Easter and got a resounding yes! I purchased my ticket. My daughter asked me if I wanted to spend time with her in Washington D.C. in the summer and I said yes! And I purchased my ticket. It doesn't matter if I'm burning through my saved vacation time, which I get paid in a lump sum upon retirement. I'll attract other resources to buy my car. What matters is that I'm there for my family, including my husband. I need them and they need me. I will find the time and resources to be there for them. Whew! I'm finally getting my priorities straight.

When I was approached to write this chapter, everything in me was screaming no! First, I didn't have a compelling story, no major obstacles to overcome, and, second, how would I find the time? I've learned a lot from taking on this project.

I've learned a lot about myself and what has made me who I am. I've cried more than once as I was writing this story, but the experience has also been exhilarating and liberating. A few quotes from Jen Sincero's book *You are a Badass: How to Stop Doubting Your Greatness and Start Living an Awesome Life* sum up the other lessons learned. "Because so often when we say we're not qualified for something, what we're really saying is that we're too scared to try it, not that we can't do it." I was petrified! I struggle with opening up to anyone but those closest to me. How could I bare my soul for all to see? In the end, I just trusted that this opportunity had been given to me for a reason. How could I not take it? "If you're serious about changing your life, you'll find a way. If you're not, you'll find an excuse." (Jen Sincero) The same applies for any goal or challenge one is facing.

I agreed to write this on December 17th but didn't start writing my story until six weeks later. I finally shoved my doubts and fear out of my brain, rearranged my schedule and got started. This endeavor has shown me that I can find the time for things important to me. I now need to make that same commitment for other goals I have in my life. "Nobody ever accomplished anything big or new or worth raising a celebratory fist in the air from their comfort zone." (Jen Sincero) Writing this chapter has definitely taken me out of my comfort zone. It has also given me so much joy and has taught me a lot about myself. I want to continue challenging myself and get out of my comfort zone.

The journey is about what you realize and what you decide to do about it. We all have parts of our lives that aren't perfect but if one is ready to grow and expand one's horizons, the key is to want to make the needed changes. As I'm evolving from changing my motivation from necessity/certainty to possibility, my search for finding ways to motivate and inspire others will continue. This will entail further learning and growth, as well as finding ways to give back more. I want to unkink my hose, a process that Peta Kelly describes as removing anything from your life that is blocking your life force. I want to be me!

I'll end with this quote from Jen, "You're on a journey with no defined beginning, middle or end. There are no wrong twists or turns. There is just being, and your job is to be as you as you can be. This is why you're here. To shy away from who you really are would leave the world you-less. You are the only you there is and ever will be. Do not deny the world the one and only chance to bask in your brilliance." In the end, I feel I'm an ordinary person who has led an extraordinary life. I have a lot to be thankful for and it's time to start sharing more of me, now! I'm confident that I will find more ways to do just that as I continue my journey. The possibilities are endless, and I'm thrilled with the uncertainty of that. Wait, uncertainty? Yes, I no longer need to be in control of every aspect of my life. I'm ready to follow the path that unfolds before me.

“Beautiful are those whose brokenness gives birth to transformation and wisdom.”

~ John Mark Green

CHAPTER 9

Conscious Life, Conscious Death

By Michell Mercer

When my friend Geraldine asked me to be with her at the end of her life, little did I know that it would be the greatest gift I would ever receive. Four months later, I used these gifts to help my sister Debby as she passed.

Geraldine was a flamboyant soul. An artist and poet. I met her through mutual friends. When I found out she had breast cancer, I offered her free Holistic Pulsing sessions and she took me up on that offer.

Holistic Pulsing is the Body-Mind therapy incorporating gentle rocking and stretching that helped me overcome virus-related illnesses-Ross River Fever and Epstein Barr. For years I had chronic fatigue, fibromyalgia, and depression. Holistic Pulsing releases physical and emotional trauma from the body. I went on to become a Practitioner and

Teacher of this therapy. It's called Power of Softness, as its nurturing and soft but deeply powerful.

At first, Geraldine would arrive at my house on her push bike full of life, she would tell me her wacky stories of her alternative cancer treatments. She watched her mum go through the same spiral and decided it was not for her. She opted to face this battle head-on using only natural therapies. This didn't sit well with her friends who were afraid of losing her. But I believe that life is ours to decide how we want to live it. This is what drew her to me, my non-judgement and acceptance.

She was on all the best diets, receiving alternative treatments from healers. Documenting her journey as she went. We worked together over the next few months and the sessions were deep. Although her body was healthy, the tumors in her breast kept growing. There were times when she felt hopeless and other times confident. Sometimes, the tumors would shrink and other times they would grow. Holistic Pulsing made her relaxed and peaceful. I felt honoured to be part of her journey.

During our session's she was able to let go of past hurts and find acceptance in her condition.

After a while she drifted off to try other things. I didn't see her for a few months but when we did meet, she would share her latest attempts to "beat this bastard".

She gradually started to lose weight and the tumours burst through her skin, an open wound developed on her breast. It was around this time that she asked me to be part of a team. We were three women who would nurse and help her face this part of her life. Every third day, I would go to Geraldine's house and stay with her through day and night. There were friends who came around - making food, doing the housework, and bringing flowers. But she didn't want visitors, she only wanted us. We administered her drugs, made her comfortable, listened to her as she came to terms with death. Each day she would be writing in this little book. She had written every item she owned and allocated each piece to a person she loved. As time went on, the journey became harder. She was in a lot of pain but refused to be fully sedated. She wanted to remain as alert as possible.

She had been to the hospital once to have her lung drained - a horrible and painful procedure. It was filling up again so we had to take her back, much to her disgust, to have this procedure done again. It was during this time that we arranged a Buddhist monk, llama Tenda, to do a blessing. I drove to Byron and picked him up. I remember thinking how strange it was to be in a Catholic hospital and having a Buddhist Blessing.

We got back home after the procedure. As the wound on her breast grew, we tried other means to combat it. We procured medical maggots to help eat the rotting flesh. But they would die immediately and the stench was unbearable.

Eventually, it was Manuka honey that helped the most. The nurses helped us shower and dress her but she would never let them touch her wound.

After a few weeks, things had gotten worse and we had to put her back into the hospital. She wanted to die at home but her condition had deteriorated, we couldn't look after her at home. We stayed with her at the hospital. After a bad night, Geraldine decided she had enough. After much discussion with the doctors, nurses, her family and carers, a decision was made to give her a cocktail of drugs that would put her to sleep until she took her last breath.

Before the drugs took hold, I asked her if I could perform gentle Holistic Pulsing as she was slipping into unconsciousness. I gently laid my hands on one knee and rocked her until she was asleep. The next day she took her last breath.

The Buddhist tradition on death is to sit with the body in silence after the person has died, allowing time for the soul to pass. Geraldine requested we do this after her death. We then washed and dressed her. We finished with her hair and make-up. This is where I realized how beneficial performing these tasks were in helping me come to terms with her death. We were involved in every aspect - decorating her coffin up to the crematorium. All these experiences came in handy when four months later I did the same for my sister, Debbie.

Deb had cancer of the spleen and had it removed. But she relapsed after a course of radiation treatment that didn't work. This was one of the most painful experiences of my life - watching my sister die. She wanted to be at home when she died and we were able to do that for her. My journey with Geraldine had given me the tools I needed to help Debbie have a peaceful passing and help her kids be part of the process.

The night she died we sat near her bedside, telling stories of our life with her, sometimes laughing and sometimes crying. I'm sure she heard all of it. Her death came at 2am. I was devastated but relieved that she was no longer in pain.

After she died, I helped everyone be part of the process - washing, dressing, and putting on her make-up. We sat with her body in the morning until the funeral home arrived to collect her.

This was the most intense time of my life but the most rewarding. Assisting someone, as they die, is the most humbling experience I've ever had.

After my sister died, my youngest daughter left home to travel overseas. I decided to move into Queensland to live with my mum and dad. They had not been coping well. Dad was starting to go downhill health wise. He was taking care of mum as she started having emphysema. In between the time Geraldine and Debbie died, dad had a major operation after his gallbladder burst. He hadn't recovered well. The stress of losing my sister was a major blow for both of them. And so, I moved in with them and became their carer.

I didn't think that I would be spending six years of my life doing this. But these experiences defined who I am. The next two years were focused on dad, as his health declined. I slowly took over his role in the house, doing the cooking and cleaning. I took them to their appointments, tended the garden and looked after their dog Zac.

My life was focused in making their last years happy and comfortable. People are amazed I had given up my life to do this. I thought, "They looked after me when I was little so it was the least I could do to help them." Dad's wish was to be at home when he died, and I was able to grant his wish. The last two months of his life were hard. He developed a melanoma on his arm that eventually killed him.

Some days, I would lie in bed with him as he opened up about his life. I realised we were alike in many ways which I had never noticed before. We shared the same sense of humour. During this time I was able to deal with the issues I had with him. I'm grateful that we had this time together.

My dad drank a lot when I was growing up and I grew to hate him when I was a teenager. When I was young, I wanted a dad who adored me. But he was so damaged by his own childhood that he drowned himself in alcohol. As a child, I never understood that and blamed him for not being present. Spending time with him, as his life was coming to an end, gave me the opportunity to receive the love I always wanted to get.

It was amazing to watch him come to terms with his life. He would call each of us to spend time. He talked about his life. He apologised for his drinking and not being a good dad when he was younger.

As the days grew near he would say to me, "I can't believe I'm still here, I didn't know how hard it was to die." We would laugh about it. I was telling him each morning that it's okay to let go. It changed my mind about euthanasia because I know if dad had the means he would've taken it. It was in the last weeks where he was able to process his life and have the opportunity to say sorry.

The morning before he died, the nurse helped me wash and dress him. I laid with him and gently told him that I would look after mum and we would be okay. An hour later I left to see a friend, take some time out. I was out for thirty minutes when my brother called me to say that he thinks dad is dead. Mum was on the verandah when I got back home. She was confused but quickly realized what had happened.

There was a feeling of relief and sadness. He died at the age of 85. It was easy for me to accept because I knew that he had lived his life to the fullest. My brother and I performed the same duties as we had done for my sister, washing and dressing his body. This last act of kindness was the least we could do for him.

Mum was finding it hard to cope with the loss of dad. In the space of two years she had lost her daughter and then her husband. After 59 years of marriage she was now on her own. A few months after dad died, I took mum to South Australia where she grew up. I thought it would be good for her to reconnect with her sisters and revisit home. She had a great time. She showed me the school she went to and the houses she lived in. She spent hours talking with her sisters about their lives when they were kids.

Her father was very strict and mean. I helped her process her childhood issues. She was confused as to why she had been sent away to live with her grandparents between the age of two and five. After talking with her sisters, she found out that her mum had post- natal depression. Her mum was struggling to cope with three kids and another on the way. Having been a counsellor for years, I helped her understand her emotions and let go of her anger and resentment.

Over the next year we took a few trips. We went to see the whales as a highlight. We did a day trip out from Mooloolabah, on the Sunshine Coast of Queensland, and were lucky enough to have a big pod of whales come swim around and under the boat. Mum was thrilled to see them so close, they were coming right up and eyeballing us. We had good times over the next year and I'm glad we took the opportunity while she could still travel. Eventually she became more incapacitated with emphysema and ended up on full-time oxygen.

I was starting to feel trapped and couldn't see the end date to this caring gig. One day I found myself talking to a friend, he owned a café with his parents. Things weren't going so well. He was looking for a partner to buy out his parents share. For some crazy reason, I decided to buy them out. Little did I know that the next three years will be the most stressful years of my life. It was a lesson on partnerships.

I eventually bought my friend out and ran the café on my own. A family member had offered to lend me money and this was another lesson. I got the money with no strings attached, knowing that I couldn't pay it back until I sold the café. I had a lot of work to do for that to happen. Unfortunately, it caused issues in the family. I realised that I had put myself in a position of no power. Falling back into being a scared little girl, feeling helpless and victimized. When I realised that I wasn't a little girl and I had the power turn around the situation, I worked long hours and kept going until I paid back the money. I vowed never to put myself in that position again.

When I sold the café, I took a break and visited Bali. I hired someone to take care of Mum. I booked my ticket and took three months off. Resting and rejuvenating my tired body and mind. Although I was having a break, I was still on duty. Mum was in and out of hospital during this time. Cas, my friend, was present in the hospital helping take care of her. She would send me updates regularly.

I came home after three months in Bali. I wanted to spend some time with mum. The extra care I arranged for her was going well and so after a month I decided to return to Bali. I knew she wasn't happy but I needed to have some time on my own and prepare myself for what was ahead. After a few months, mum was again in hospital. I knew that I needed to come home to stay.

I managed to get her home from hospital and we spent the next few months going out for walks at the seaside, buying her favourite gelato and making happy memories. I'm glad I got to spend the last couple of months with her.

Christmas was coming up and I bought a Christmas tree with lights and decorations. I knew it would be mum's last Christmas. I helped her wrap presents and write cards. She was excited - we started to plan the food and what we would do.

Two weeks before Christmas I went to Melbourne to attend my daughter's graduation. After that, I went to the Gold Coast for my other daughter's baby shower. The day before I came home, mum picked up a virus. When I got home, I started her on the antibiotics but I think it was too late. They didn't seem to help.

I called her specialist Dr. Samantha, who had been looking after her for the last four years. She asked me if mum wanted to go to hospital and mum said no. We did our best to look after her at home. The next two days she got worse and was struggling to breathe. I asked her again if she was ready to go to the hospital, this time she said yes.

Dr. Sam organised a bed for her at the private hospital and the ambulance arrived to pick her up. I stayed with mum through this time and eventually Dr. Sam arrived to see her. The first thing mum said was that she's had enough and she couldn't continue. I was a bit taken aback. I hadn't realised we were at this stage.

The next morning when I arrived, she was doing better. She wanted to talk to the grandkids. By the afternoon, she seemed to have gone downhill. We had talked many times, over the last years, about her death and now she had decided it was time. We sat together and she told me she was tired. She was ready to go and join dad in heaven. I felt sad but I knew but this was her decision to make.

That evening when Dr. Sam came. Mum once again told her that she was ready. She had enough. She couldn't go on any more. Dr. Sam said that she knew mum wouldn't say this if she didn't mean it. Dr. Sam said that we could put her on drugs that would help her sleep. Slowly, with no food the body would start to breakdown.

The drugs were started and mum went to sleep, but she kept waking up. She was still in pain and they would give her more. They seem to work for a few hours and she would wake again. Dr. Sam kept increasing the dose. It didn't seem to matter how much she had, she would still wake up after a few hours.

The next day was Christmas. We brought all the presents and some food for us to the hospital. Mum slept most of the time but woke up to ask us if we liked our presents. She was determined to have Christmas with us.

I talked to Dr. Sam on the phone that night telling her the drugs weren't working. As if mum developed immunity to them. Dr. Sam replaced them with morphine. I gave mum a big kiss and said my last goodbyes. I knew that she will not wake up again. After she fell asleep, I went home to get a change of clothes and then joined Cas's family gathering at Golden Beach. I was restless to stay long.

When I got back to the hospital, my brother and sister-in-law were sitting beside mum who has not woken up since. My brother, who didn't want to be there when mum died, and he left with my sister-in-law in the afternoon. I spent the next few hours sitting with mum knowing it was our last time together.

By six o'clock in the evening, Cas and our friend Kate arrived to sit with me. Dr. Sam joined us until nine o'clock. While we talked quietly, I noticed that mum would miss a breath now and again. When Kate and Dr. Sam left, I knew that mum didn't have much time left. Cas and I sat on both sides gently applying Holistic Pulsing at her knees.

What happened next was beautiful, my hands were turned over to face upwards. It felt like her soul was placed into them, gently lifting her up and out of her body. She took her last breath and was gone. It was peaceful. I knew that she was happy at that moment.

I called Greg and Kennen and they came to help me wash and dress her. I felt a sense of completion — to be with my parents, sister, and friend as they took their last breathes. Now, it was over.

We had a beautiful ceremony for mum who didn't want a big funeral. She had all the details planned out down to the music — Queen's 'Bohemian Rhapsody' and Van Morrison's 'Bright Side of the Road' — to the bright colored clothes we'd wear to celebrate her life. We gathered - her children, grandchildren, great-grandchildren, friends and family to say goodbye and celebrate her life. Kind words were spoken about her, and tears were shed. It was everything she wanted for her funeral.

I would like to offer words of encouragement about being with your loved ones in death. In the past, people cared for their loved ones at home when they died, but at some point, we gave this power over to mainstream funeral homes. We've become afraid of death. We don't want to look at it. We send the body and never see them again. Being involved is not for everybody but if it's something you might want to do, I want you to know that we have legal rights. We can spend time with our loved ones after death. We can hold them, wash them and dress them.Time gives us the opportunity to come to terms with their death. It makes the process gentler. Separating ourselves from this process robs us of the opportunity to honour our loved ones. This helps us in our own grieving process.

Throughout the past eight years, I haven't really taken the time to grieve. I always seem to be moving on to the next one. I thought that when mum dies, my tears will come pouring down. But they didn't.

I grew up in an era where it wasn't acceptable to show your emotions. We were told to get over it, stop crying and be a brave little girl. And so I learnt that it wasn't ok to cry or show sadness. I would always hear this voice telling me to be strong. Of course, over the years I did cry. I would stop myself quickly and have a massive headache afterwards. As a child, I retreated inwards and created my own world. My parents both worked so I spent a lot of time on my own. I had low self-esteem and didn't believe I was worthy of being loved.

The beliefs I formed when I was little stayed with me as I grew up and I kept creating situations to validate those beliefs.

But I always seemed to have a keen sense of the undercurrent and hidden agendas of people around me. I learned my lessons easily, knowing that I was guided from above. Despite the many challenges that life gave me, I trust that the universe would provide everything I needed.

I never had a good relationship with men in my life, I was looking for the love I craved from my dad. As a teenager, I entered into many relationships. I never knew what it was to be on my own, I got married at the age of nineteen.

My first husband was a gentle soul. We had a lovely relationship and we are still good friends to this day. We share two beautiful daughters and tried our hardest to make our marriage work but after 10 years together our relationship ended.

I started a new relationship straight away with another guy and went on to have a relationship with him for 20 years. We had one daughter together. Our first years together were very happy but soon, the cracks started to appear.

I ruined these relationships because I was scared of being hurt or left, so I always kept a barrier up. Its only in hindsight that I can see that.

I ended my second relationship to be on my own for the first time since I was a teenager. This is what I needed to find inner peace and happiness.

I have spent the last thirty years doing self-growth and learning therapies. When I came across Holistic Pulsing and Voice Dialogue, this is when I was able to see my own patterns of behavior. I discovered limiting beliefs I had formed in my lifetime. I started taking responsibility and took my power back. I now use these therapies to help my clients release their past hurts.

A testimonial from one client

"From the moment Michell placed her hands on me I felt safe, I could feel the energy that needed to be released. My visuals increased and I was able to access parts of my childhood memories - good ones and bad ones. Michell's nurturing made my experience comforting. The energy release was amazing, after the treatment I felt more connected to myself. It made me relaxed and more aware."

I create a ritual every new moon and full moon. They help me create the life that I want. I use them to release pent up emotions I have, things I no longer need in my life. Then, I invite and wish things for my future. I concoct a new ritual every month depending on what I'm dealing with - either I'm struggling with my body image, being judgemental to other people, or trouble deciding how to move forward with my business. These are the basis for my ritual. Rituals help me introspect and gain clarity. I see changes needed to achieve the life I want.

A few years ago, I realized that whenever I talked about my sister, it was about her death. Telling the story allowed me to hold onto her. It was if the 56 years we had spent together, ceased to exist and that her dying was all that was left to talk about.

I decided that it was time to let go and create a new narrative to help me get better.

This is how I did it.

I set an altar with flowers, crystals and a beautiful amber pendant that she had given me before she died. Then I ask for guidance to let go of the despair I have. I acknowledge the gifts that helped me become who I am today. Telling myself, "From this day, I no longer see myself as sad and broken by her passing but healed and whole, able to feel compassion and unconditional love for myself and others. I am now richer from this experience. I know she will forever remain in my heart and that we are now one with the universe."

I then wrote a letter for her, which I later burned while chanting an ancient Tibetan Buddhist blessing. "May you be filled with loving kindness. May you be well. May you be peaceful and at ease. May you be happy."

The last part was an exercise of self-affirmation — to honor and treat myself with love and respect. Remind myself of my power, knowing that my thoughts create my world. I begin each day with the words 'I am enough' which I had tattooed on my arm as a daily reminder.

I've learned over the years that when we refuse to accept our situation, it creates a lot of pain and anguish. If we can come to a place of acceptance it can make life and death a lot easier. Resistance is something that comes up a lot when I'm working with clients. It is usually fear of the unknown. We would rather stay in a bad situation than take the risk to change.

It's easier to let go of the negative emotions we carry every day than to hold on to them. We go through life holding on to the past, our childhood beliefs and behaviors because we think it's too hard to let go. We're not sure of what life will be like without them.

Often, years of intense therapy or counselling doesn't help. By using self- reflection you may see what it is you no longer want and what no longer serves your highest good. Acknowledge it, let it go and move on with your life.

When I first came to Bali seven years ago, I promised myself I'll live here for at least one year of my life. Now here I am. To create this reality, I've had to jump into the unknown many times. I'm not saying it was easy but I did it anyway. The biggest lesson I have learned from the past seven years, caring for my loved ones as they died, is to live life each day as if it's your last. Don't be afraid to do the things you want.

When I left my second relationship, it was scary being on my own for the first time. I wasn't sure if I'd done the right thing but somehow in my heart I knew it. I needed to do this to find myself. Buying the café was a leap into the unknown. There were times where I questioned my sanity. But I know that it was a lesson I needed to learn.

All these experiences led me to grow in many ways. I no longer see myself as a victim but a powerful woman creating the life she wants. I have the ability to make decisions without knowing the outcome. I trust that I am being guided in the right direction.

I have been brave to look at myself and make changes to become who I am today. I still stumble, sometimes, but I know I have the tools to pick myself up and keep going.

I know that it's not always easy but I wanted to show you that you can. It's not as hard as you might think. Taking responsibility for yourself and your actions gives you the freedom to create a rich life. Make your dreams come true, hold on to them, and don't give up.

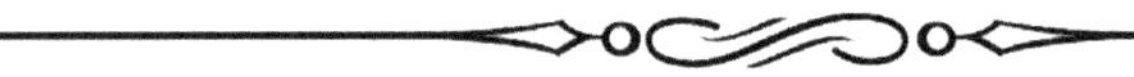

"Transformation is not a future event. It is a present day activity."

~ Julian Michaels

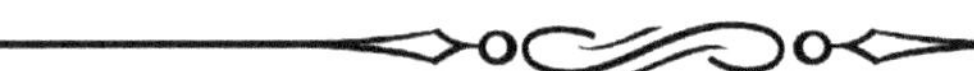

CHAPTER 10

Inner Compass

By Annina Brühwiler

How I revealed my inner compass

I am focused. I'm a hundred percent in this very moment. I am, everything. My heart is beating, I am full of adrenaline, and I can hear my blood flushing through my veins. The landscape just flies by; I don't know what is going on around me. The only thing I see is the road and the next corner which I'm approaching at full speed. One wrong move and I'll end up sliding over the asphalt. My legs hurt, but I have never felt so powerful before. I'm mastering it. My body and mind can deal with more than I could ever imagine. All the sorrow, fears, and struggles of my life are blanked out. Rarely have I experienced that before. I'm bombing down the four-kilometer-long track on a hill somewhere in Czech Republic. I am wearing a full-face helmet and a turquoise leather suit similar to motorbike protection gear. But I'm not on a motorbike. I'm standing crouched on my longboard, an item through which I learned so much over the past 1.5 years. This is my very first downhill skateboard race. This is in summer 2017, eight months before writing these lines. And this is a pivotal moment of the story I want to share with you.

If you'd asked me two years before, I would never have expected spending my summer by pilgrimaging from one longboard event to the next. I hadn't thought that I would learn something completely new and sophisticated within that time period and make friends for life through sharing a passion. I hadn't thought that I would be more courageous and venturesome in my general decision-taking and living. However, I did, and eventually revealed my inner compass.

Childhood: A little bit of everything but nothing serious

But let's turn back the clock a little further, back to the time when I was in primary and secondary school. I was a smart kid, never got into trouble, was living the storybook childhood. I was energetic and had many hobbies. Too many, as some people would judge it. Monday tennis, Tuesday piano lessons, Wednesday artistic gymnastics, Thursday giving private lessons in mathematics, and Friday I was certainly busy as well. Every year I tried out a new hobby: ballet, volleyball, floor ball, swimming, aerobics, and hip-hop dancing, just to mention a few. However, I never felt fulfilled by those activities and gave up soon after starting.

Snowboarding was one of the sports I kind of liked. However, I was discouraged because everyone around me learned new tricks faster. I decided that I was not made for snowboarding in the snow park and doing some crazy flips over jumps. I thought I wasn't made for something extraordinary and just cruised down the slopes like everyone else. My brother, instead, practiced skiing with an intensity and motivation I only discovered years later. Every free minute, he would grab his free-skis and try out new tricks with his friends, building kickers in the snow for hours, flying over and over it again just to step up the slopes afterwards. How many times have he and his friends failed, trying double back flips and other crazy stuff like an immense professional kicker? Again, and again. I was fascinated and amused by my brother's persistence, by his commitment, by his smiling face even after a crush or after hours of exhaustion. Still today, my brother follows his passion and shares it with the next generation. He's now a ski instructor.

As for me, I think I never knew what it meant to be passionate about something. I had multiple interests, multiple talents. I tried out many things, enjoyed them for a while and then dropped them again due to a lack of satisfaction. I remember one moment when I was around 12 years old. My school organized a freestyle sports day as part of a sports encouragement project for children. I chose slalom skateboarding. In one afternoon, I learned the basics of pushing, pumping, and braking with a skateboard. It was my very first contact with skateboarding and longboarding, and I loved it.

Unfortunately, there was this nasty voice in my mind telling me that this was only something for boys. I was rather boyish and hated all the girly pink glitter, Barbie dresses, and make up stuff. I preferred playing with Legos with my two younger brothers or rolling in the mud in the forest with my cousins. Yet I thought skateboarding was for the cool kids only. And it is something you have to get started with when you're seven years old because you could never catch up later. Don't ask me where I got this mindset from. It's sad enough that it was strong enough to pull me away from this sport. The more time passed, the more I lost the motivation and confidence to get started. It is incredible how, especially as a kid, we are influenced by gender prejudice. And as you get older, you realize it's only a dogma and yet more powerful and influencing than you might imagined. On the other hand, if the Universe (how I like to refer to the Divine) wants you to experience something, it lets you come across one theme again and again until you get the hint and begin to follow the signs. And so I started following it.

Coming of age: Stroke of fate

Nevertheless, I had to learn it the hard way before I could free myself from many dogmas, beliefs, and fears. I was always convinced that in every life there is a moment when everything gets shaken up like from an earthquake or volcanic eruption. When you get hit by fate, you're forced by external circumstances to open a new chapter in life and transform your personality.

It was on an ordinary Tuesday afternoon in 2007. I was 15 years old and about to start high school four days later. What had happened then was one of the reasons why I was stuffing my days full of studying, sports, and other activities that were fun yet not fulfilling to me. It was part of a survival strategy to keep me distracted. Still a kid, I took too much responsibility for my younger brothers and my mom. I lost track of what I loved and what was good for me. It was the reason why I try to please everyone and why I wanted to be loved by everyone through performance. I was ambitious and successful. I was the best pupil in the class and participated in every project I could. Nevertheless, I had to learn to listen to my gut again, to do things for myself and not for everyone else. Furthermore, this experience is also the reason for many fears I'm still trying to overcome, still to this day, namely the fear of opening my heart towards men. All of this because I was abandoned by the first man in my life. I was abandoned by my dad.

This particular afternoon, my dad, who was a healthy, strong, and smart man, had a brain hemorrhage. Days, nights, and weeks of sorrow followed. He was in a coma. The prognosis was disillusioning: if my dad would ever wake up again, he would never be able to walk and speak. More than 10 years later, I can say my dad is fine. He's living in a care home, is able to walk on crutches, can vocalize names and lyrics, and recognizes everyone. He is still my dad and always will be.

And I am infinitely grateful for my mother and how she dealt with the situation. A therapist herself, she taught me how to learn the most from this lesson which my soul wanted me to experience. Through her, I discovered the path of self-development which I have followed for 10 years now. The most important thing I learned is, everything happens for a reason. We are not to ask for the Why but for the Wherefore. Everything we experience is only as bad and as sad as we allow it to be. We can always change our perspective and look on it from another angle. We're responsible for our own happiness only and not for the people around us.

Of course, I didn't learn this within two weeks; it was a process over a few years. And I'm thankful for all the ups and downs I have had so far. The whole situation brought me closer to my two brothers and my mother. And still now my father can proudly live his role as my dad. My mother takes him to every concert, school ceremony, and birthday party.

So, I lived an ordinary life like every other teenager, struggling with the decision of what to study, falling in love for the first time and being heartbroken only a few months later, travelling with friends, acquiring my first work experience from several freelance jobs, having the first hangover after partying all night long, getting tired of that and focusing on work. After becoming a radio host at the age of 21, something I'm extremely proud of, I decided to study communication and journalism. It was a good choice, and I would definitely do it again.

During those years of wandering about and searching for my calling, I saw a skateboard in a shop and I remembered this workshop when I was a kid. That day, I finally bought a board and started cruising around in the city. However, I didn't try to pop an ollie or to skate on the mini ramp. I kept telling myself that I was too old for that. My mind-monsters, as I like to call my self-sabotaging thoughts, had control of me. I got some hints from life again to follow this path of longboarding and skating. This was the beginning of a life-changing journey, of a new mindset, of revealing my inner compass. (Maybe it is difficult to comprehend these lessons from the perspective of longboarding or skateboarding. If so, just think about something else that fulfills you in life, because the learnings might be the same for you.)

Lessons Learned Through Longboarding

1. You're never too old to learn something new

One week in Portugal with 15 other highly motivated skaters. All women. It was my first Women's Longboard Camp back in 2016. I discovered it on Facebook. I took that opportunity and booked the camp and the flight. It was the week of my 24th birthday. On my flight there, I was convinced that I was going to be the oldest girl in the camp, awkwardly trying to get more confident on the skateboard while all the teenagers around me learned in one day what I had to work hard for months to do.

This mind-monster was actually from my snowboard lessons back in the day. I was surprised and relieved when I met the other participants. The range of ages and backgrounds was astonishing. Doctors, architects, mothers, therapists, teachers, researchers, up to the age of 50, complete beginners to semi-professionals. And there was me: a student, inspired by all the other women – and by far the youngest! Not only in this camp, but also in the other three camps that took place in the following two years, the atmosphere was just inspiring. Being among like-minded people, learning from others, sharing the experience, teaching others, and—the most important thing—sharing a passion no matter what level of experience or skills.

This experience awakened my desire for learning also in professional terms. Within a few months, I learned how to set up a website and how to use photoshop. I learned not only downhill longboarding but also skating in skate bowls and mini-ramps. And if at the age of 30 I feel like learning to dance Tango or at 40 I want to learn Arabic or at 60 I want to climb mount Everest, I'll just do it. Everything is possible. The same is true for you. Don't limit yourself. Follow your impulses, ideas, and dreams. You don't have to be great to get started. You have to get started to be great.

2. Sharing is caring! It's about the community

I'm walking up the hill for the estimated 153rd time this day. The sweat is running down my forehead, the sun is burning, I'm carrying my board with my right arm. I can't communicate with most of them because of a language barrier. This doesn't matter. We all have a huge smile on our faces and loads of fun practicing some slides on a street corner underneath palm trees with an ocean view. I'm the only girl and the only white person on this skate session in Lombok, Indonesia.

How did I end up there? I was on holiday in Bali and googled longboarders in Indonesia. It turned out there is a big longboard community. Even though we had only connected on social media, from the first second we met they treated me like an old friend, not like a stranger. The guys didn't have much to share, but what they possessed, they shared with me. Why did I always want to have the latest gadget or clothes when it is just enough to have a secondhand skateboard and friends to share the passion with?

I instantly hated the strive for possessions in western countries and started rethinking my concern with material goods. I realized that I possessed much more than I actually needed and decided to deliver most of my skate equipment to the longboard community in Lombok. Those nights I slept in a hammock in the backyard of a small house without running water. Others let me stay in their rooms or lent me their bikes. From the beginning there was a blind trust. Only the fact that we're sharing the same passion opened a completely new possibility to connect with local people and to make my travels an even bigger adventure.

"What? You just go to some stranger's place and sleep there? That's dangerous!" my friends would say. I don't think so. Having something you like in common lets you connect and trust people immediately, and it will surpass gender, age, language, religion, and social status. And whoever is coming to my town, I would host him and try to return what I have been given.

Sharing a passion, be it chess, programming, travelling, or cooking, makes it easier to connect to and trust those like-minded people. It requires an open mind and a basic trust in humanity. Of course, you should always use common sense and listen to your gut feeling. All the more, I'm grateful that all those encounters and experiences with longboarders, be it in a faraway country or in my hometown, reaffirm my attitude towards strangers. Most of the time, you can trust them, and you'll be rewarded!

3. It's only as dangerous as you decide it to be

"They must be insane," is the verdict of most people when they watch a video of a longboarder bombing down a pass route on a skateboard. It's true: this is a f**king dangerous sport. What if a car comes out and hits you in the corner? What if the street is slippery and you end up in the guard rails, rocks, or down the hillside? What if the person in front loses control over the board and you crash into each other? What if...?

I admit, there is always this "what if." It's dangerous. Everything is dangerous. It depends on your perspective and on how much responsibility you take for your actions. Because, like in every situation, you can reduce the risks to a minimum.

Longboarders don't unreasonably risk our lives. We take calculated risks. We always wear protective gear: knee and elbow pads, slide gloves, helmet, and back protector. For big events or races, a full-face helmet and leather suit is mandatory. I can say, I wouldn't be alive anymore if I didn't wear my helmet without fuss or quibble. If we are skating on a public road, we send a car ahead to give us information through mobile radios about upcoming cars and the condition of the road. Even then, we always make sure to stay in our lane and to ride within our limits. A great opportunity to push our limits are free-ride events. There are hay bales in every corner and a marshal keeping the track clear and safe.

From the outside, this sport might look extremely dangerous. However, it's not! There is a difference between doing something imprudent and taking a calculated risk. Imprudence can cost you your life. The latter is the area where you learn the most about life, about yourself, about your limits, and about how to overcome fears. It's the one and only way to leave your comfort zone and go where the magic happens.

4. Listen to your body

Me and my body have always had a rather difficult relationship. I was always sporty and fit. However, I was not skinny and muscular. And even looking at a cupcake made me put on weight at my hips. When I was a teenager, I often felt uncomfortable in my body and I wanted to look like the pop stars and actresses in the magazines.

Today I know that it's not about how you look but how you feel. And I feel comfortable, even grateful for my body. I ask a lot from it. After intense skate sessions, I might have road rashes and bruises, sprained or twisted ankles or wrists. That's part of the game. My friends are already used to seeing me approaching slightly stumbling or with a bandaged forearm. However, I wouldn't say I'm acting unreasonably. The opposite is the case. Those smaller accidents and injuries made me learn to listen to my body, to accept when I needed a break and get more sleep.

And I started to give my body something back. Now I do regular stretching similar to yoga, attend to my body and do energy-based therapies, and I meditate. I recharge the battery, let the energy flow, and heal myself from inside. My attitude is that our body is like a mirror of our mind. I don't get a headache by chance. My body wants to tell me something, whether it is through an accident or a disease. There is no coincidence. Every physical issue—be it cancer, a heart attack, a stroke, a migraine, or a broken leg—is rooted in a mental or emotional stress or lack of attention. This is why I believe that, if the Universe wants me to step back and rethink the situation by letting me break my leg, it has to happen anyway, no matter if I crash with too much speed in a corner or stumble down the stairs.

In order to learn that, I first had to crash a few times. And now I have an early warning system. It's my knee. On one event, I screwed up in a corner. I had too much speed for my skills and I ended up in the hay bales. But first, I fell with all my weight on my right knee. Nothing broken, nothing twisted, but a very badly bruised bone. "Okay, I thought. If you don't want to respect your limits, you have to learn it the hard way."

But it was only half of the lesson. I didn't give my body enough time to recover. Three weeks later, there was the next event. My knee still hurt and wasn't ready to race. I ignored it, so I got cursed with another stupid, inevitable crash. This was two lessons in one. First of all, the energy follows your attention. All day I was worrying about falling on my knee again. In every delicate situation I imagined myself landing exactly on my already injured knee. Therefore, I was bound to hurt my knee again. This phenomenon is also known as self-fulfilling prophecy.

The second lesson was to recover completely before getting on track again. This time, I accepted the hint and gave my body a longer rest. This was six months ago now. Sometimes my knee still hurts; it's a slightly painful throbbing. However, it does not hurt when I'm skating, not when I'm dancing fulfilled all night long, and not when I'm having sex. It only hurts when I'm working at my desk or lying in my bed.

Then my knee is telling me: "Be more mindful with your body. Take a rest. Don't focus on work only. Practice awareness. Take a deep breath. In and out. And be grateful for your body. Because you only get one body per life. Treat it accordingly."

5. Do it for yourself

When I was in high school, I wanted to join the army. I wanted to prove to the world that I'm strong enough to stand the highly exhausting drills. Always seeking affirmation and attention, I wanted to have the best marks in school, the best results in sport competitions, the best performance no matter what it was about. I was a perfectionist. I never wanted to join a team for sports, because one of the team members could have been better than me, something I couldn't stand. There is nothing wrong with a competitive, ambitious mind. If, however, it has self-destructive traits, it's a bad thing. It took me many years and some therapy sessions with my mom to overcome my self-destructive perfectionism and doggedness.

Today I know I don't need to prove anything to anyone. And it's not about being better than one specific person. It's about me getting better than I was before, improving my own skills, and having fun. Done is better than perfect. I'm glad that I reached this state of mind before starting long-boarding. I'm not doing it to show the boys that I'm a tough girl. Okay, admittedly, a little bit, yes. But mostly because I love doing it because I discovered something that makes me happy and I've never seen the other skaters as opponents or rivals. Even when racing, it's not about beating someone else but beating my best time. Seeing someone mastering a skill motivates me even more. Spotting only the back of the other skaters in a race pushes me to my limit and a little beyond. Instead of trying to beat each other, we should support and inspire each other. Be it sports, art, or work, everyone should just give the best of themselves so that we can mutually motivate each other, get better, and grow.

6. It doesn't matter how many times you fall (as long as you get up again)

Someone might just watch me practice longboarding and think, "How stupid is that!" For example, when I'm learning a new kind of slide...this is like squatting on the board and touching the asphalt with one plastic puck on my gloves and sliding on this puck and the four wheels at a right angle to the street. This skill is essential for racing and braking on the track. As one can imagine, I didn't learn it within an afternoon. In a practice session I might fail 80% of my tries and fall. Sometimes I land on my kneepads, sometimes just jump off my board and land on my feet, sometimes do a somersault, sometimes land on my hips, twisting my ankle, scraping my underarm or hitting the back of the head. Sometimes it hurts, but most of the time, it just motivates me even more. Sometimes swearing but mostly smiling, I get on my feet again, wipe the dust off my clothes, and walk up the hill and try again to slide in the corner. I want to master that sh**. And I know it's possible to master because so many people have done so before me.

In some ways this might sound familiar to you. However, most of us are more familiar with another situation: We want to do something new, but after five or even 10 or 20 attempts we decide to quit. We believe that we don't have enough talent, that it takes too much effort, that we would never make it to where our heroes or idols had made it. We keep telling ourselves that we are incapable of doing it. But is it really talent? Or isn't it rather endurance and persistence? It can be summarized in the 10,000-Hour Rule. Malcom Gladwell claims in his book, *Outliers,* that the key to achieving world-class expertise in any skill is mostly a matter of practicing for a total of around 10,000 hours. Be it bowling, writing poems, programming, or skating.

There is one example of trying something, falling down again and again, and still getting up again that everyone knows: learning how to walk. As a toddler we see that walking on two feet must be possible. We stand up and try to make some steps just to fall again and again. If we would do it with our mindset of today, we might give up after a few attempts, telling ourselves that this is too difficult for us and we don't need it anyway since we can crawl around on the floor. Nevertheless, as a toddler we keep trying to walk because we know that walking on two feet must be possible since we see it done every day by the people around us.

The examples stated above should encourage us to not give up too quickly, knowing that if we fall down, be it literally or figuratively, we should just get up and try it again. The more we fall, the less it hurts. I know this from my own experience. Surprisingly, over time the body gets used to crashes and the subconscious mind knows how to react to make it as harmless as possible. And as your body gets used to physical fails, so the mind gets used to the mental ones. With every fail we get better. Just get up and try it again. And again. And soon you will master it, whatever it might be. It just starts with the first step.

7. Live the moment

Too often, my mind is chattering around. For Instance, while having a coffee with friends, while working, while reading a book or even while having sex. I lose control over my mind; I am at my mind's mercy. You know the state of flow in which you are fully immersed, focused on something and enjoying the activity? I have often heard about it but rarely experienced present-moment awareness. Some exceptions are after an hour of intense sports, after physical exhaustion, when the energy of a chattering mind was needed in other zones of the body. For years, working out was the only way to stop thinking about yesterday and tomorrow and be in the present, at least to some extent. Meditation or yoga? I wasn't patient and persistent enough to reach a state of inner silence, of experiencing the present.

That is, until I discovered slacklining as a hobby a few years ago. The goal is to walk on a tight rope which is set up around 50cm above the ground between two trees. The more I was able to keep my balance, the more I realized that this is also balancing my mind. I learned what it meant to live in the moment. When I stood on the slackline or carefully put one foot before the other, trying to compensate the shaking with my arms, there is only me and the line. One thought like "I should do this or go there" would make me lose my balance and fall off the line. Through slacklining, I experienced for the first time what it meant to be present, to be in that very moment and not to think or worry about anything else. I found my way of meditation.

Similarly, I am there when I'm longboarding. It's obvious: I don't have any choice. Racing or just bombing down a street at 70 km/h is indeed a risky thing. Thus, not being focused, not being in that exact moment, can cost you your life. As initially described, on the track, for the duration of a few minutes, I'm a hundred percent focused. Since that intense focus is required during the descent, it's easier to keep it upright on the way up again, be it in a car or walking. And even after a skate event of several days, after a day trip to a skate spot, or even after an evening or after a work session, I feel free. My mind has slowed down. I'm beaming with joy. I'm grinning at every person I come across. Now, being familiar with this state of mind and the feeling of experiencing the moment, I can provoke it more easily within other activities, be it at work, while having dinner with friends, listening to music, or just sitting on a bench and enjoying a sunset. Just take a deep breath and enjoy the moment.

8. Magic happens outside your comfort zone

This quote might be overused and sound flat. However, everyone knows, at least deeply inside, that this is true. Why does it take so much to leave our comfort zones and try something new? Quit the job and finally go on a world tour, tell someone "I love you," talk to strangers, or dig into your deepest personal fears? Longboarding showed me that the quote "magic happens outside your comfort zone" is true in two dimensions.

Firstly, through longboarding, I learned to leave my comfort zone in the first point. It's impossible to improve yourself if you are too afraid of falling down and getting hurt, be it literally or figuratively. This is what namely holds us back from taking important steps in life. Therefore, knowing that the more you fall the easier you get up again, and that the more your body and mind get used to it, made it easier for me to leave my comfort zone in skating and longboarding.

In addition, I learned that, as most experiences in life, it's a matter of perspective. Sometimes, after a session with 14 fails or crashes, I'm much more fulfilled than when everything has gone smoothly. When I crash, I know I risked something. I left my comfort zone and tried to improve my skills, not being afraid of the consequences. That fills me with pride and joy. And still the lesson about leaving the comfort zone is broader, more comprehensive.

Thanks to that immediate experience in skateboarding and longboarding, I became braver in other dimensions of life, especially in my professional life. The events came thick and fast in the previous months and yet were always for the best. Since I was no longer paralyzed by making risky decisions (admitting, I'm still scared sometimes), I finally started listening to my inner voice, to my heart.

It's not a coincidence that the initial step for my current professional situation had been made during that longboard race event in Czech Republic. I was on holiday from my internship in communications and marketing in Switzerland, a job I liked although I wasn't really thriving. It was the last month of my five-month internship, and I wasn't clear whether I could continue working for this company afterwards, nor was I sure whether I actually wanted to, either.

During that skate event, my boss called me and offered me a well-payed full-time job with a lot of responsibility and flexibility in the agency. Most of my friends would probably have said yes immediately and considered me unreasonable because I wanted to think about the offer again. The more I thought about it, the more convinced I became that I was not yet ready for settling down and starting what people would consider a serious life with a safe income in a stable environment. I, however, was pulled into faraway countries again since my thirst for adventure had not been stilled yet during the five months of travel prior to my internship.

Safety is a construct of our minds anyway. So, I took some deep breaths and a therapy session with my mom. And then I left my comfort zone. I refused the job. I was back to square one. But I was proud of my step. I was fulfilled, and I knew that there would be something more to come, and there was. Luck was on my side and the main theme was skating and longboarding.

To make it short, two months after refusing that job offer, I was living in Bali, Indonesia, and working part-time for a local skate park whose boss and crew I'd gotten to know during my previous travels and also part-time remotely for the company in Switzerland that had offered me the full-time job. When I would go back home two months later, I could continue working there with a 60% stint as I'd asked for. Everything turned out better than I had expected. As one could imagine, I was perfectly happy. Life wanted the best for me, and all just thanks to the moment when I left my comfort zone.

I would definitely do this again. I recommend everyone to leave their comfort zones every now and then. That doesn't mean you have to start with quitting your job, but maybe with taking a cold shower every morning. I do it every day and I can promise you, the prickling and the awareness of your body is worth it.

9. If I was inspired, I can inspire other girls

My exciting journey started about two years ago, that time I was inspired by a small community of longboarding girls. Retrospectively, it was no coincidence at all. It was all meant to be and was meant to happen. Yes, I needed several hints until I finally devoted myself to that sport which turned out to be my passion. I needed some kicks to my posterior. There might be many similarly thinking girls out there. And it's exactly those girls I want to motivate and inspire. For now, my goal is to motivate other girls, no matter what age or background, to finally step on a skate or longboard. To overcome their fears and dogmas and to win against their mind-monsters, to practice persistence and the art of falling and getting up again, to experience joy, the feeling of togetherness, the new power of a new mindset. Therefore, when I was working in that skate park in Bali, I established weekly girls skate sessions and worked for free as a skate instructor for girls.

Probably, most of the skating teenagers in the park would consider my skate skills as beginner, at the very most intermediate. I can't blame them. It is true. However, my goal is not to teach them any new skills but to teach complete beginners some basics, give them a helping hand, and to inspire them. My project was successful. Regularly I was rewarded with happy faces. Sometimes we were up to 12 girls in the park, above average for every skate park. I was rewarded by smiling faces, by "thanks for helping me overcoming my fears," by seeing the girls giving each other a helping hand or advice, and mostly by girls telling me something like, "You know, all my life I have been fascinated by this sport, but I've never been brave enough to get started. Now I finally did it."

After my return to Switzerland, I was happy to see that the skatepark kept on organizing the girl skate sessions even though there wasn't a host or instructor. It filled me with joy to hear from my friends there who told me that the girls kept going to the park and connecting with and helping each other. Mission completed, this one at least. The next is just about to start. The sports encouragement project for kids that brought me in contact with longboarding for the first time 14 years ago contacted me. They asked me whether I wanted to work part-time as a female long-board/skate instructor for their school projects. And so, this circle closes. I'm convinced some girls will discover their passion. Maybe one day one of those girls will even give skate lessons to the next generation.

10. Revealing the inner compass needs time

I used to be worried about not knowing my purpose in life, not having a calling, not knowing what I wanted to do. Over time I learned to accept that. It's okay to not know your calling or your purpose in life. It rarely happens that, as a child, you know exactly what and who you want to become in life and end up there straight away. As for me, thanks to long-boarding and skating, I discovered my inner compass, not for my job yet, but at least for my hobby. It changed my mindset, which will definitely have a positive impact on my career and other areas of life. My goal is not to make every human start longboarding or skateboarding.

This is definitely not everybody's thing. Even if you found your inner compass, there might come days of disillusionment, of sorrow, of doubts. Again, it is your decision whether you want to wallow in self-pity or you step into action. In difficult situations there's a simple way to keep your head above water: writing in a happiness journal. It consists of writing every day at least three things that made you happy, proud, grateful, or that made you laugh. There are many positive aspects about acquiring this habit. First of all, it changes your perspective and you start to focus on the positive things that happen in life. Secondly, soon you will recognize certain patterns in your journal. This will help you to discover your passion, in case you haven't detected it yet.

As for me, every skate session is in my journal, every crash I didn't get hurt too much, along with good grades on exams, a nice chat with friends, friendly encounters with strangers, something new I've learned, or an important decision I have made. Thirdly, soon you'll realize, no matter how crappy a day has been, you will always find three things to write into your journal. I've been doing it for five years already, and, seriously, every day I find something. Extrapolated, there are more than 3,000 entries in my happiness journals. This practice will help you to see life from a brighter perspective. Last but not least, if you are familiar with the Law of Attraction, you will just attract more positive, fulfilling situations into your life. What we focus on expands.

From Retrospect to Outlook

It took me a while to reveal my inner compass. It is still not fully developed. At least, I finally understand why my brother, with his passion for skiing, could spend hours and hours in the snow, ever ambitious to learn a new trick and to accept failing nine out of 10 times. Now I pass my free time with like-minded girls (and boys) in the skatepark trying a new trick on the mini-ramp or with my longboard on a corner in the quarter practicing some slides.

I'm more than ready for the next longboard and race season with travels all over the world for some skate trips. I'm ready to speed down streets, get out of my comfort zone, maybe get hurt, knowing I will always stand up and try it again. I'm ready to live in the moment, to listen to my body as well as to my gut and my heart. I'm ready to learn something new every day, to be grateful for every experience. And I'm ready for my life!

“Knowledge + Understanding = Wisdom
Wisdom + Application = Transformation”

~ Unknown

Author Autobiographies

Chapter one

Rod Hairston

CEO and Chairman of Growth-U

Rod Hairston is one of the fastest growing authorities in the area of organizational culture, leadership and human potential. Rod has coached leaders to Forbes's 400 list, star athletes and organizations like Disney, ABC and Honeywell and is the creator of the 45-Day Challenge® series, which has been internationally recognized as one of the best integration programs for change.

Rod is a dynamic speaker and author of the highly acclaimed book *Are You Up For The Challenge? Six Steps to Lasting Change, Starting Now...Not Someday.*

Early in Rod's career he received his certification in NLP and NAC and spent several years as a Master Trainer for Anthony Robbins, where he then created his own coaching business. He is also the mastermind and creator of the most intelligent, sophisticated and simple conditioning system in the world. This online coaching system continues to reap great results for several companies in 19 different nations.

For over 20 years he has helped more than 500,000 individuals expand their identities and over 500 companies change, enhance and create high performing cultures. He is an avid believer that: "The life you have, you've created – with your thinking and emotions." One of his sayings is: "what's hard to do in the beginning is easy to live with in the end," and believes that a person should be most concerned with the habits they create for their life.

Chapter two

John Spender

John didn't learn how to read and write at a basic level until he was 10 years old. He has since traveled to more than 45 different countries, started many business's leading him to create the award winning book series *A Journey Of Riches,* he is an Award Winning International Speaker and Movie Maker.

John was an international NLP trainer and has coached thousands of people from various backgrounds through all sorts of challenges. From the borderline home-less to wealthy individuals, he has helped many people to get in touch with their truth to create a life on their terms.

His search for answers to living a fulfilling life has take him to working with Native American Indians in the Hills in San Diego, the forests of Madagascar, swimming with humpback whales in Tonga, exploring the Okavango Delta of Botswana and the Great Wall of China. He's travelled from Chile to Slovakia, Hungary to the Solomon Islands, the mountains of Italy and the streets of Mexico.

Every where his journey has taken him, John has discovered a hunger among people to find a new way to live, with a yearning for freedom.

He also co-wrote the script for the film *Adversity* and interviewed all the guests.

John now lives in Bali, where he runs his publishing business from his lap top.

Chapter three

Alex Hoffmann

Millionaire Networker. Author. Speaker. Coach. Dad. Athlete.

For over 25 years Alex is known as a Distinguished Strategist, Business Architect, and Multi-Millionaire in the Network Marketing profession. Alex is one of the few Networkers who has succeeded in this profession twice as a distributor, and as a corporate executive. Since 1993 he has been one of the most influential Networkers in the industry in Latin America and US Hispanic, both as a distributor and as Regional President for two top companies. Alex is originally from Venezuela, considered a Multicultural Hispanic American, who has lived in Mexico for five years and now is a US citizen that has lived in the US for more than 20 years. He has traveled the world more than two million miles, visited more than 40 countries and over 200 cities in which he has trained more than 100,000 people.

Alex holds a Bachelor's degree in Business Management and a Master's degree in International Marketing from Brigham Young University. Alex has several different personal development and coaching certifications from the top authors in the world like Stephen R. Covey, John C. Maxwell, and Anthony Robbins.

Alex's greatest passion is sharing quality time with his kids and traveling around the world. Alex is a high performance athlete who enjoys cycling and marathons in different parts of the world, from Patagonia, Berlin, France, Spain, Miami, among others. He has completed more than 30 competitions between Marathons, Half Marathons and Centuries (100+ miles) in cycling. Alex's vision is to transform the lives of thousands of families in Latin America and the Hispanic community in the US by offering them freedom through the Network Marketing profession.

Chapter four

Katie Neubaum

Katie is the mother of three beautiful children. She received her BA in Vocal Performance from the University of Miami and completed her graduate studies at the University of South Carolina.

She is a very successful professional Network Marketer. She is known as "Linkedin Girl," and has a monthly webinar to teach others to leverage social media to create wealth.

Katie is also an International Singer with a focus on Jazz and Classical repertoire. Her production company, Find Your Greatness was established in 2013 to provide a gateway for talented artists of all ages to perform in their chosen field of excellence. She served four years in the United States Army as an Intelligence Analyst.

Katie practices the Laws of the Universe and she believes it is possible to have, do and be anything you truly desire. Katie acknowledges her connection to God source energy, the angels and believes that something magical is always happening.

My Linkedin

www.linkedin.com/in/katieneubaum

My website

www.findyourgreatness.today

My Facebook

https://m.facebook.com/kneubaum?ref=bookmaks

Chapter Five

Noelani Love

As a Native Hawaiian mother, designer, singer/songwriter, yoga teacher and ocean lover, Noelani Love creates to inspire.

Love dedicates her art of music and jewelry design with the intention to radiate love into the world. She is humbled, yet inspired, by the grace and courage of humanity, the creative and destructive aspect of nature, and the strength of our spirits to continually evolve.

Love spends her free time surfing or freediving, hiking in the forest, cooking with her 10 year old son Aukai, playing music, and reading. She loves to learn!

Her work serves as a reminder that we are all inter-connected through this home, our earth, and through the spirit of creation.

In addition to sharing her iconic jewelry line and sacred music around the world, Noelani leads international retreats, women's moon circles, and sound healing ceremonies.

Find out more at www.NoelaniHawaii.com

Chapter Six

Jeanetta Matichak (Jeana)

Jeana is a Christian woman, mother of three crazy kids, married to an amazing man of God. She feels she is here to help others learn from their experiences in life.

Walking through the valley of darkness she found herself. Jeana is a self-help coach and loves to help others find God and love their life. It is only when you have experienced the darkness that you truly love the light.

Learning how to transform has been her biggest adventure and deepest struggle. Jeana loves to read, run and spend time with her family. She sends her love and light to all her readers.

Jeana is also the author of *Finding Peace* and she plans to write many more books in the future.

Chapter Seven

Gemma Castiglia

Gemma is passionate about all aspects of life, including evolution. She has managed to flip her life and bravely delved deep within her experience and life lessons.

Gemma's empathy, gifts and her deep emotional connection to energy, the Universe and creation, has journeyed her back to her true-self and now continues to dedicate & empower her life through her own life lessons and experiences and her vast years of self-development and esoteric studies and clinical education. To Holistically Healing the Body Mind

Heart and Self; Amalgamating Energetic and Clinical Modalities to be up there with the best to assist in Wholly' Balancing and Integrating a person who is ready to Transition, Transform and step into the best possible version of themselves.

"If we go deeply within and clear our past negative emotions such as anger/sadness/fear/anxiety/guilt/ hurt and Refill/Reboot/Reintegrate our energetic body, this enables us to experience A new beginning of Life'.

Chapter Eight

Elizabeth Palmer

Liz is from Arizona, married to her husband Tom for 32 years, they've raised three amazing children, Wally and Alyssa who are 26 and Erica who is 31. She has worked overseas in developing countries for the past 28 years and during that time visited over 50 countries. Liz currently works in Germany for a regional office that supports countries in the Middle East. She is also a professional trainer for financial management professionals in the Agency that she works for.

Prior to her current job, Liz worked in the private sector as a Controller and prior to that for a Certified Public Accounting firm. She holds a B.S. from Arizona State University in Accounting and Computer Information Services, and is a Certified Public Accountant.

Liz is currently on a personal journey of growth and development. She is seeking ways to use her talents to give back more to others when she retires in two years.

Chapter Nine

Michell Mercer

Michell is an Intuitive Energy Healer and Change Facilitator. She is a qualified Teacher and Practitioner of Holistic Pulsing, a Voice Dialogue Facilitator and connects to spirit using these modalities as well as cards, crystals, and ritual to guide her clients on a nurturing journey of healing, self-exploration and transformation.

Michell has been actively involved in assisting at many births and deaths over the last eight years. She has gained invaluable experience and information which she lovingly shares with others. Michell is in the process of developing a video series 'Conscious Life, Conscious Death' a guide to being present with your loved ones as they transition.

With over 30yrs experience in group facilitation, Michell now teaches Holistic Pulsing Training through "The Australian School of Holistic Pulsing" and facilitates one-on-one and group, Women's Healing Retreats in Bali and Australia.

www.relaxrelaterejuvenate.com

www.holisticpulsing.com.au

michell.mercer@gmail.com

Chapter Ten

Annina Brühwiler

Annina is 26 years old and grew up in the Swiss Alps. She's a passionate and semi-professional downhill longboard skater and travels the world to follow her passion. Still working mainly in marketing and communication, she knows that there is more in life than sitting in an office for eight hours per day.

Rather she inspires other girls to start longboarding and empowers them to follow their passion and to listen to their heart. They benefit from it for personal development by transferring the learnings from longboarding or other extreme sports into lessons for life. Therefore, she created the blog and community "Shred and explore yourself".

Annina's goal is to show that you can be a daredevil and a spiritual human at the same time. These two qualities are closer to each other than most of the people might think. Join the movement and explore the power inside you. Explore yourself. Inspire others.

FB: Annina Ninsk Brühwiler

Insta: @ninsk_on_tour

Twitter: @ninskali

Mail: anninabruehwiler@bluewin.ch

Web: anninabruehwiler.com / shredandexploreyourself.com

Afterword

I hope you enjoyed the collection of heart felt stories, wisdom and vulnerability shared. Story telling is the oldest form of communication and I hope you feel inspired to take a step to living a fulfilling life. Feel free to contact any of the authors in this book or the other books in this series.

Please help us get the inspiring messages out to people by leaving an honest review on amazon.com and lets have more people living from the mindset that you can truly do anything with this life.

Other books in the series are...

Letting Go and Embracing the New: A Journey Of Riches Book 8

https://www.amazon.com/Letting-Go-Embracing-New-Journey/dp/0648284506/

Making Empowering Choices: A Journey Of Riches Book 7

https://www.amazon.com/Making-Empowering-Choices-Journey-Riches-ebook/dp/B078JXMK5V

The Benefit of Challenge: A Journey Of Riches Book 6

https://www.amazon.com/Benefit-Challenge-Journey-Riches-ebook/dp/B0778S2VBD/

Personal Changes: A Journey Of Riches Book 5

https://www.amazon.com/Personal-Changes-Journey-John-Spender-ebook/dp/B075WCQM4N/

Dealing with Changes in Life: A Journey Of Riches (Self-help guide, Change, Motivational, Inspirational Book 4) https://www.amazon.com/Dealing-Changes-Life-Motivational-Inspirational-ebook/dp/B0716RDKK7/

Making Changes: A Journey Of Riches (Self help guide, Changes, Life changes, Change, Spiritual, Habits Book 3) https://www.amazon.com/Making-Changes-Journey-changes-Spiritual-ebook/dp/B01MYWNI5A/

The Gift In Challenge: A Journey Of Riches (Self-Help, Anthology Books, Spiritual Solutions, Mindset, Book 2) https://www.amazon.com/Gift-Challenge-Self-Help-Anthology-Spiritual-ebook/dp/B01GBEML4G/

From Darkness into the Light: A Journey Of Riches (Self-Help, Mindset, Motivation, Inspiration, Anthology, Short Stories Book 1) https://www.amazon.com/Darkness-into-Light-Motivation-Inspiration-ebook/dp/B018QMPHJW/

Thank you to all the authors that have shared aspects of their lives in the hope that it will inspire others to live a bigger version of themselves. I heard a great saying from Benjamin J Harvey and that is 'We are only as sick as our secrets' When you share your secrets you just never know who you will inspire and heal in the process.